LOVE IS FOR ALL OF US

LOVE IS FOR ALL OF US

poems of tenderness and belonging
from the lgbtq+ community and friends

edited by **JAMES CREWS** & **BRAD PEACOCK**

foreword by Richard Blanco ✦ art by Lisa Congdon

Storey Publishing

THIS BOOK IS DEDICATED to all of the LGBTQIA+ family members we have lost too soon. And to those who continue the journey of making this world a safer place where we can all love each other and ourselves more freely.

IF YOU ARE CONSIDERING harming yourself, free, immediate, and confidential help is available through The Trevor Project. Call 1-866-488-7386, text 678-678, or chat at thetrevorproject.org. Help is also available through the National Suicide and Crisis Lifeline simply by calling or texting 988.

A PORTION OF AUTHOR PROCEEDS from this book will be donated each year to The Trevor Project, an American nonprofit focused on suicide prevention among lesbian, gay, bisexual, transgender, queer, and questioning youth.

CONTENTS

HOW POEMS LOVE

At my readings, workshops, keynotes, class lectures, even at cocktail parties—anywhere I'm able to engage people on the topic of poetry—I point out that the act of writing poetry is a political act by nature, practically by definition. Even if the general intention of a poem isn't obviously political on the surface, when courageously penning thoughts and emotions, to some degree every poet is driven by a need to exercise some amount of political agency—in the broadest sense of the word—by pushing back against the status quo of their lives and of the worlds they inhabit—past, present, and future. Poets question, investigate, and aim to discover new perspectives, new emotions, and new possibilities for themselves, for their readers, and even for their detractors. This rings even more loudly, truthfully, and urgently when concerning the often-traumatic life experiences of queer writers.

However, upon reading—well, savoring—this compilation of heartful poems you hold in your hands, it occurred to me that writing poetry is just as powerfully and authentically an act of pure love writ large. We love nature when we painstakingly describe the precise color of a flower, the scroll of mountains, or the sounds/symphony of the sea. We love others when we praise, pay tribute to, or elegize the soothing gestures of their smiles, the timbres

of their kind voices, the warm empathy in their eyes. We love our lovers and spouses by rendering the shape of their hands caressing ours, by recording our simplest yet most intimately meaningful conversations with them over shared meals, by noticing the forest of their eyelashes and the tide of their bodies' breaths rising and falling as they sleep. And, perhaps most importantly, we love ourselves by loving back in these tender ways through which we look at others and the world. And—equally so—by the ways we look into the mirror of our own poems to embrace ourselves in the gaze of all our vulnerabilities, our resiliencies, and our joys, out of which our rightful humanity appears clearly in our eyes.

—RICHARD BLANCO

THE COUNTLESS FACES OF LOVE

I can still see those two young men kissing on the street that morning in Portland, Oregon. As sunlight broke through cloud cover, I watched the two of them say a long goodbye to each other, kissing and kissing again. Looking out from the window of my bus, even from that distance, I could feel the tenderness of their connection, the way they kissed without shame, no attempt to hide it from others as I might have done at that time in my life. Ever since, I've carried that small scene with me as a reminder of the right to live and love out in the open, which so many LGBTQIA+ people have fought for over the years and are often still denied. Those two men gave me the hope that I, too, would someday find someone to love, though it would be another decade before I met the man who would become my husband, before we would share a moment like that on our own first date one winter night, kissing and kissing goodbye out in the cold, as people passed by us on the sidewalk, neither of us caring for once if they saw us or judged us.

We all deserve to show our love for each other in the plainest of ways, without having to worry about threats that others might pose to our safety. This is one of the main reasons that my husband, Brad Peacock, and I embarked on editing this anthology. We have both been discriminated against for our sexual orientation—insulted, rejected, and made to feel less-than—more times than we'd like to count.

Our hope for this world is that we can all stop trying to restrict, reject, and target people for who they love or how they express their genders. As you open the pages of this book and begin taking in the life-affirming and heart-filled poems we have gathered here, we hope you enter a safe space where you, too, feel that love is for everyone, not just for a chosen few. We hope that you feel permission to become exactly who you are, knowing that you belong here.

These poems reveal, each in their own ways, the many forms love might take—romantic love, self-love, love for nature, and love for the friends and family members who embrace us as we are. This book brims with voices from LGBTQIA+ people and allies who show us how intimacy manifests in daily life, from sleeping together in the same bed to sharing a cup of tea; from doing laundry for the ones you love to picking up a spouse from the airport and kissing them in front of everyone else. In addition to poems by Richard Blanco, Ellen Bass, Mark Doty, Nikita Gill, Andrea Gibson, and other established poets, we have included a wide spectrum of emerging poets. This book also features prose pieces that explore the art of becoming and loving ourselves. We hope people of all ages will feel both seen and heard, uplifted by the stories of others that we often need to read in order to access our own journeys of becoming. Poetry has the mysterious yet undeniable power to bring people together and re-create moments of deep intimacy and connection with very few words. If poems or essays in this anthology speak to you and unlock your own stories, we encourage you to write in response, perhaps even keeping a journal nearby as you read. Every poem is like an open door, inviting you inside, and each person who enters will find something different waiting for them. Let's never forget we are here to learn from each other and our relationships, keeping an open mind and heart to the endless varieties and countless faces of love that will speak to all of us.

At a time when books are being banned simply for their content, without any regard for context, when LGBTQIA+ people are being attacked and ridiculed, with laws placed on our bodies and our right to exist out in the open, we see this book as an antidote to prejudice. We believe these poems are the exact medicine we need to help us love each other, ourselves, and the world more fully, remembering that no matter who we are, and no matter our situation, we deserve the everyday wonders life offers us. As Mary Oliver famously wrote in her poem "When Death Comes," "When it's over, I want to say all my life / I was a bride married to amazement. / I was the bridegroom, taking the world into my arms." May we all feel safe enough to seek out and receive the tenderness we need to thrive.

—JAMES CREWS

3

Married to Amazement

The man I married sat next to me
after our wedding, October light pouring in
over dusty pews as he loosened his tie
and sipped from a cup of apple cider,
closing his eyes to savor the taste.

Now I think I didn't marry *him* so much
as his amazement for the everyday,
the way he still gasps each time we see
something new—baby painted turtle
plodding through a stream in the quarry,

or a neon-orange caterpillar inching
across crisp leaves on the trail,
how he kneels to film it from every angle
while I crouch beside him, in awe
of his awe, learning all that I can.

Sleeping with You

Is there anything more wonderful?
After we have floundered
through our separate pain

we come to this. I bind myself to you,
like otters wrapped in kelp, so the current
will not steal us as we sleep.

Through the night we turn together,
rocked in the shallow surf,
pebbles polished by the sea.

She Ties My Bow Tie

What you thought was the sound of the deer drinking
at the base of the ravine was not their soft tongues
entering the water but my Love tying my bow tie.
We were in our little house just up from the ravine.
Forgive yourself. It's easy to mistake her wrists
for the necks of deer. Her fingers move so deftly.
One could call them skittish though not really because
they aren't afraid of you. I know. You thought it was the deer
but they're so far down you couldn't possibly hear them.
No, this is the breeze my Love makes when she ties me up
and sends me out into the world. Her breath
pulled taut and held until she's through. I watch her
in the mirror, not even looking at me. She's so focused
on the knot and how to loop the silk into a bow.

Why Pour Water on Us at Night?

I want to collect your heat
in my hands, tend it like
the logs on this fire. I want
to sit in this blue chair in
Fuller Park, watch your white flames
dance across pink water
at dusk. I want to rest here
beside you, absorb the blaze,
pause to gather more heat,
then stoke you
for the rest of my life.

The Secret Is That the World Loves You

When no one was noticing, you tucked twenty dollars
    into the hand of a stranger asking for change.
And there was fluttering when you expected floodwater,
    a guardian angel with her hand on your hip
while you spun satellites in your mind until the universe
    went full tilt, planets pinballing. The world loves you—
how you smile at sticky children, how you hold the door open
    for people you've never met. Some days it's almost too easy
to be helpful, to make a million friends because you don't spray
    pesticides across your lawn—the grasshoppers and cocoons
thank you. We're hanging in there, knowing love is love is love
    and also temporary, like us. And while you sometimes exist
in highwater jeans, you aim to unwind with hibiscus, hollyhocks,
    anything that gives you a little buzz, since you adore
the honeybees, alive and humming in sync with the cliffswallows
    who returned with the pair of goldeneyes floating across
the lake—they're still together another year, seasonal monogamy.
    Like all of us were that summer when everything fluttered,
and all those afternoons, the monarchs landed in your hair.

Migration

Last night when you lowered your body down
on top of me, I thought of the monarchs
at the tops of pine trees in Mexico.
It was high in the mountains.
I'd been gone from home for a long time.
I stood in the pine forest and listened
to the thick body of those butterflies.
Heavy in the trees. The limbs
clotted as with snow. Monarch on top of
monarch and the outer wings shifting
to keep position. Some sort of pulse in the trees.
As if breath itself had taken on a body.

PAUL TRAN

Enlightenment

You illuminated me.

We see what we believe.
We believe what we see.

I close my eyes to open them.

Here's a lamp.
Here's oil for the lamp.

From me to you.

On a Hill at Night in a Chair under Stars

A face at the window. Doves
floating down from the eaves.
He drifting off. No stars.
A parliament of owls roosting
in the branches. By morning
there were flowers everywhere.

Open

Not seeking anything
along the morning path,
I see the many clusters of
"false" goldenaster spread over
the field like constellations.
These the world would call
weeds, would tear up
before noticing the way
each flower opens, stands
in the early light like a small
yellow palm, like the hand
of someone who, after
so many years of looking
and waiting, longing deep
and far, has at last made peace
with what the world is
and is ready to take
what it can give.

On a Pink Moon

I take out my anger
And lay its shadow

On the stone I rolled
Over what broke me.

I plant three seeds
As a spell. One

For what will grow
Like air around us,

One for what will
nourish and feed,

One for what will
Cling and remind me—

We are the weeds.

Just the Wind for a Sound, Softly

There's a weed whose name I've meant all summer
to find out: in the heat of the day, dangling pods hardly
worth the noticing: in the night, blue flowers . . . It's as if
a side of me that he'd forgotten had forced into the light,
briefly, a side of him that I'd never seen before, and now
I've seen it. It is hard to see anyone who has become
like your own body to you. And now I can't forget.

Softly

Everything I see returns to you—
ice melting down muddy worn footpaths

as gray April days slip their way into May,
the goldfinch arriving after a season of sleep.

I breathe out winter's forgotten dreams,
still see your eyes in the flowers.

Bittersweet is all that's left since you decided
it would be sunnier on the other side.

There is no getting over, no moving on.
There is nothing to be fixed, only to be carried.

I'll carry you like I am learning to carry myself—
softly, one day at a time.

Love,

Though I am undeniably broken,
I come to you with no need to be fixed.
I come to you the way one river
meets another river—not joining
out of thirst, but because
there is so much power
and beauty in giving oneself
to another, in moving
through the world together.
I come to you the way the half moon
comes into the yard—I could be more
whole, but in the meantime,
I will bring you everything
I have.

Intimacy

It is the bee
dipping itself into the slender cup
of a morning glory,
one hidden inside the other.
It is the way water
gentles its body against river bank.
It is the hawk hugging itself
into wind,
thermal holding the bird like a hand.
It is the expression on your face when
you first noticed me,
before I knew your touch like my own.
The day your eyes took me in
like a shelter,
loving before even knowing why.

Watching the Bees in the Asters with Grace

Summer turning over her leaves,
the fennel no longer succulent for picking
but full of yellow flowers pulsing in a final show.
All the small creatures buzzing, the miniature magicians—
the fat bumble and the wild Italian honey
flashing their fancy wares. The tiny mason bees
and the nameless others I call natives—
though she doesn't know what that means.
She tells the story again of how she got stung
but didn't cry "because I like the bees" she says.
She repeats this over and over, touching her arm
in the place where she wears an invisible badge.
Is she tough enough?—she is trying to ask.
Is she tough enough to let the wild things sting
and still love them a little? Grace,
reaching for the fennel, reaching for the fig,
reaching for the lemon balm, the sprig
of lavender, for the hot-lips sage blossom to devour
with her own tongue, reaching
for my palm, for my palm, then past it
—for the terrifying dazzling beyond.

TENDING

by Kai Coggin

My hands are in the earth around our koi pond, pulling back the winter blanket of leaves from the edges and through the crevices of all the rocks and boulders that hang over the lip of the water. My heart whispers, *Wake up, sleepyheads, time to grow* to the small sprouting friends. I pull back the dried leaves and see a carpet of purslane and the small green swords of yellow irises pushing up like backward Excaliburs of spring, bordering the edge line. Our four fat koi fish swirl in their orange white yellow hues, shimmering with morning.

Up in the garden across the way, my wife is spinning what she calls *thorny devil vines* around the trunk of a young black cherry tree to prevent the black rat snake from twirling up for a breakfast of eggs. The familiar bluebird couple has come back to the house that's strapped to the tree—the third year in a row, the family home where they will have their babies. All over the property, clinging to trees, are the houses my wife has put up for the wild ones to call home, some proper builds she made with scrap wood, some hollowed-out dried squash apartments that once rattled with seeds, now emptied with a door and natural warmth.

I, too, am a wild one who calls this home now—my life before this was so cold, so empty, and now I am bathed in such a natural organic warmth. This life. This life with her, 16 years of loving each other fiercely, tenderly. The seasons that we grow and grow and grow together. Now spring is approaching. The sun just broke through morning clouds. I don't know how many more seasons we will have together—27 years between us. It'll catch up to us one day. But not yet.

I wish that I could let everyone see through a window into this tender life, see the fruiting body of our love bloomed from everything we planted in the darkness, all the light we strive to fight toward together. I never expected this life. If you'd have asked me as a teenager, I would've said I didn't really expect to live past being a teenager, could never envision what a home really felt like, what love really meant, what partnership and family could become—until she opened the door, and I was on the other side. And we haven't looked back since, through hell and high water, sickness and health, grief and joy. So much joy.

I'm so thankful for these days, for every hillside, every sprout, every flower in spring, every fallen oak leaf in the winter that covers our land in crisp brown. I'm thankful for the birds' songs in the trees—not just for the harmony of them, but thankful that together we know each individual song by heart, the red-bellied woodpecker, eastern bluebird, cardinal, junco, tufted titmouse, the hummingbirds' whirring chitter. I could catalog all the species our love has poured into, here at home. I could encyclopedia the days, the trees, the buds, the seeds, the flowers. I just never thought this was possible, but now my hands are covered in the soil of our earth, covered in the home that we have shaped with our life. I have dug my feet into the soil that is underneath my fingernails—every atom of this land has merged with mine, my body merged with hers. There will never be a goodbye here. I will feel her here forever. This will always be our home, the sweetest years of my life, the most creative, the most tender. This morning, she's across the way about 100 yards off, doing her own tedious, beautiful work of spring, her hands in the same sweet earth, covered in the rich soil of us.

In the Middle of Our Lives

for Anne Elizabeth Parker

Warming light of my life,
imagine my days without you: desolate and alone.

No sun through our lake house window, no
Sunday French toast, you in your olive sweater

ready to shovel a path after the long storm.
Who would help me with my snow pants, or lace my boots?

How could I tell of the woodpecker, upside-down
at the feeder, or the cardinal on a bare branch

if it weren't for the way you whisper *honey*
and my eyes open, dawn of a new day.

Here, in the middle of our lives,
a parking lot kiss or knee-deep walk through a Nor'easter,

with racquets and swimsuits in a gym bag we share,
you are all I want under moonlight, wolf moon or crescent,

or when fog forms over the lake and the day goes gray and moist.
You are all I want when the sun breaks

and the difficult world goes easy,
sound of summer songbirds

flames of lilac and gold from our garden.

Sweet, Sweat

East along the line of apple trees on Hawley,
the skin of the petals translucent in the sun, early,
the body and arms of the trees gleaming through.
I come closer and press my nose into the blossoms,
the fragrance of your skin, faint sweet sweat, as if
salt and all the minerals of the earth are called
up into you and alchemized by you, breathing out
through every pore what you've lived, your love,
your chemistry, your history, the smell of your skin.

king the color of space/tower of molasses & marrow

I hear music rise off your skin. Each hair on your arm a tiny viola.
A wind full of bows blows & all I hear is the brown

hum of your flesh, a symphony of pigment too often drowned out
by the gun songs & sirens. Don't listen to that music.

You are the first light in the morning, the dark edge of the sun.
You are too beautiful for bullets. You, long the poster child for metal

wrecked bodies, are too precious for the dirt's greedy teeth.
You are what was left when the hot, bright stars danced

with the black endlessness around them. You are the scraps
of the beginning, you are not meant to end so soon.

I want to kiss you. Not on your mouth, but on your most
secret scars, your ashy black & journeyed knees,

your ring finger, the trigger finger, those hands
the world fears so much. I am not your enemy,

not poison, not deadly sin, not ocean hungry for blood,
nor trying to trick you. I came from the same red clay,

same ship as you. You are my brother first, my lover
second & never a God. I am sick of people always

calling us Gods. What God do you know that dies this easy?
If I believed in fire, I would think you a thing scorched

& dangerous & glowing. But I no longer believe in embers,
we know you can burn down with no flame for miles.

So thank you. Thank you for not fading to ash & memory.
Your existence is so kind.

The Boy & The Blue Bird

I want to see your secrets,
the things you've hidden up high
& out of sight.

Little bird,
let my autumn shed your tree,
let me lay down its thistle crown
of crimson leaves.

I wish to see
   your nest,

sacred chapel of twigs & grass,
the place you go
when you seek retreat
from song & sea-sky,

hidden home
in which you rest,
undress,
confess your sins
when no one else
is watching.

Breathing You In

The scent you say is no scent
rises from warm ports
between neck and shoulder.
Scent that isn't
witch hazel, vetiver, camphor, lemon,
but is just your skin,
raises a breeze on mine, unpredicted
as freshness I found in woods
where a few blond leaves hung from twigs.
Sweet sharpness,
scent of something still to come,
something soaked in—
chlorine on the cedar deck your thigh presses,
foot drifting in water,
eyes yellow amber behind closed lids.
Soaked in like sun
in the river whose cold silk
wrapped your body in August,
opened dark folds around you.
Closed, opened, around you.

Good Morning

Here in the holy quiet
at the sloping edge of morning,

your eyelashes rest
contented with your face

like tired shepherds, travel-weary
and hopeful after a day of goodness,

knowing once again
that all the sheep are cared for,

that your heart has spent its daily strength
on love and wonder,

and that it will seek
those hills again tomorrow—

today, once the sun
has summoned you.

Golden Hour

You chose a tattoo like the sun
for your fortieth birthday
and I wondered—
do you know that you are sunlight,
lit from within?
And that I feel warmed
when standing next to you?

You told me that when you fly
you worry the earth will lose track of you,
that she will not know where you are.
Later we learned the term for this: Place lag.
But you exert a gravitational pull
the earth herself must feel—

you the grounding force,
yours the golden hour.

what to love when you're running out of things to love

Pick any landscape—a kitchen counter, a waiting room, that part of your body
you shield from photographs—and narrow the distance between you. At first,
the stains will monopolize your eye. Each blight and crack and overgrowth,
a seismic disruption. If you can bear the stillness of not looking away, if you
step even closer, the contours will begin to lose their meaning. The noise
of an old story will fade. New shapes will emerge, like petals after a hard rain.
I'm not saying you will desire, suddenly, the pits and pores of the world,
or that your hands passing over every rough surface will feel fresh tenderness.
But you'll notice your breathing has softened, your heart a door you can open
past the jambs. How there's room for what you see, and everything you can't.

The Wait

I waken to your hand
holding mine,
you, on the floor by the bed,
the morning after I said
we are through.

Your tender vigil coaxed
the buds of love to sprout again
after the dormant season,
when I had ceased belief
in anything but grief.

Because

Because we didn't
give up
when my words scorched
like hot coals,
when your eyes were empty
as a dark hallway,
when trust was as fragile
as a moth's wing,
because we didn't
give up,
each kiss, every glance
became our home.

Goodbye Kiss

He kissed me goodbye
Right in the airport lobby in
Traverse City, Michigan
High up the west side
Of the Michigan mitten
Planted a kiss on my mouth
He didn't care who saw us
He was acting in the world
He wants to be living in
Not the world where that
Might have been a
Dangerous thing to do
But where it was normal
To kiss your lover goodbye
When he is leaving and
You're not sure when
You will see him next.

Two old men in love
Saying goodbye in
A small airport lobby
As if there were
No one else around.

Red-Eye Out of Atlanta

I'm waiting with our bags when you emerge
from the men's room, gliding as you do, effortless
across that rough sea of 3 a.m. faces.
Perhaps it's the jet lag. Or that I'm sleep-deprived
and still drunk on new love. But your hands, wet
from the faucet, your fingers glistening beneath
the dull hum of that airport light, glint
of the ring I placed there, and suddenly
I'm pulled forward the way a slow barge might
be drawn through a narrow canal, tugged along
behind you through that slough of sleepwalking
bodies. Feeling what, exactly? Safe? Yes. And happy
when you take my tired hand on our next flight,
and our next, holding it until I close my eyes.

Flight Paths

my first birthday in the city
arrived with an overdue gas bill

so my love snuck me
up the fire escape
to a wild, secret beach
overseeing all of Brooklyn

even at two in the morning
our backs were warmed
by yesterday's sun
held for us in the black pebbled roof

rum in red cups
we watched shooting stars
take off from JFK and LaGuardia
dreaming of all
the places we would go

pink sand beaches
tea in Tokyo
opera Down Under

but as an early arrival circled
the city sunrise
a breeze tickled our bellies
with the question
of home

Coming Out

I knew when the small plane I was riding in
touched down in the fog.
I knew watching my stepmother's hands
work the rock garden behind the house.
I didn't want the circle to close.
I couldn't see myself in the dress, so shaven.
I knew because I loved to move through water—
the way it yielded
the way it took me in its mouth.
I knew watching our fox hound
when he slipped out of the leash—
how he tore after a scent down our shady street.
I just wanted to sleep in the wild strawberries
with my chopped off hair.

WAVING

by Astrid Newenhouse

The forsythia is waving at me. Swaying, snow-laden, branch architecture on full display. And waving, distinctly waving. I am looking out at a winter snowstorm, and as soon as I see the forsythia, I sense my mother's presence. This plant grew from an offshoot of hers. It's hardy, unstructured, and can get messy— the first shrub to bloom bright yellow in the spring, but somewhat wild with a will of its own. It also makes a good cut flower in a glass vase in the house, bright and lively.

Years ago, together, my mother and I dug the little sprout from her yard and put it in a borrowed bucket. I drove it north and planted it here. It reminds me of her—an immigrant, adventurous, accepting. Decades ago, when I wrote letters to the editor about queer politics here in the Midwest, I used "Forsythia" as one of my pen names, afraid to be outed.

The world is different now. I'm older and don't care as much about how others perceive me. It seems more important to connect with each other, as layers of collapse happen in our world and social interactions reveal so much anger. The forsythia has grown large and given me offshoots of my own to share with friends. My mother is gone now, and we scattered her ashes in several meaningful spots in the natural world on two sides of the Atlantic. But I'd have to scatter ashes over the entire universe if I were to choose places that remind me of her love. I never had to use a pen name with her. And I can see her waving.

Tin Bucket

The world is not simple.
Anyone will tell you.
But have you ever washed a person's hair
over a tin bucket,
gently twisting the rope of it
to wring the water out?
At the end of everything,
dancers just use air as their material.
A voice keeps singing even
without an instrument.
You make your fingers into a comb.

Enough Music

Sometimes, when we're on a long drive,
and we've talked enough and listened
to enough music and stopped twice,
once to eat, once to see the view,
we fall into this rhythm of silence.
It swings back and forth between us
like a rope over a lake.
Maybe it's what we don't say
that saves us.

Small Love Poem

I have nothing
to say to you.
Confronted
by the immensity
of loving you,
I am silent as the moon.
I understand nothing.
I have words
for nothing. I know
only this:
with your face
between my hands
every moment
in which I am utterly silent
I am blessing something.

Love Poem

Speak earth and bless me
with what is richest
make sky flow honey out of my hips
rigid as mountains
spread over a valley
carved out by the mouth of rain.

And I knew when I entered her   I was
high wind in her forest's hollow
fingers whispering sound
honey flowed   from the split cup
impaled on a lance of tongues
on the tips of her breasts   on her navel
and my breath   howling into her entrances
through lungs of pain.

Greedy as herring-gulls
or a child
I swing out   over the earth
over and over   again.

Fall Song

It is a dark fall day.
The earth is slightly damp with rain.
I hear a jay.
The cry is blue.
I have found you in the story again.
Is there another word for "divine"?
I need a song that will keep the sky open in my mind.
If I think behind me, I might break.
If I think forward, I lose now.
Forever will be a day like this
Strung perfectly on the necklace of days.
Slightly overcast
Yellow leaves
Your jacket hanging in the hallway
Next to mine.

Darling

The days fall out of your pockets one after the other.
Soon you'll need a new jacket with tougher leather

and seams no one has felt. Soon you'll bring
the old books into your bed and sleep easy

and alone. It must be December again.
This must be the part of the story where you

refuse to say how the bodies you've walked toward
continue walking in you. With heavy black boots

in a calm procession of *darling* and *honey*—
they walk up and down the narrow streets of your heart.

Reel

Maybe night is about to come
calling, but right now
the sun is still high in the sky.
It's half-past October, the woods
are on fire, blue skies stretch
all the way to heaven. Of course,
we know that winter is coming, its thin
winding sheets and its hard narrow bed.
But right now, the season's fermented
to fullness, so slip into something
light, like your skeleton; while these old
bones are still working, my darling,
let's dance.

Bonneville Bathtub

The wrinkles at the corners
of your eyes are proof
that some of the nicest things
take time. Like taking the time to walk
around the block after dinner
the way that old neighbor couple does
sometimes. You know who
I'm talking about. Hand in hand,
wearing big sunglasses, taking small steps
in their walking shoes
as the sinking horizontal
light of a tired day would slowly,
slowly fill the shade inside
their wrinkles. For a golden moment
they are ageless. Because what is a wrinkle
without a shadow to condemn it?
I'm sure they'd tell us, if we asked,
that the fountain of youth is just a valley
shaped like a bathtub that fills
with copper light at ten past six
every evening. And dusk is just a squinting
reminder to keep you seeing things
clearly. The wrinkles at the corners
of my eyes are proof that the nicest thing
you gave me was time.

Ordinary Evening

beginning with a line by Tony Hoagland

We would give anything for what we have,
though it's easy to forget while swimming
in our own good luck, like that cartoon duck
I once loved to watch backstroking through
his vault filled with treasure and coins.
Someday, I know I'll stand at the counter
of the pawn shop of loss, bargaining for
just one more ordinary evening of walking
with my husband after work, our boots
scuffing gravel roads softening into spring,
and a flock of redwing blackbirds trilling
to each other in the upper reaches
of a tree we pass beneath, barely noticing
those golden notes pouring down
all around us.

Look Deeper

From outside appearances,
I may be a middle-aged man now
with gray in my beard, hair receding like an ocean tide
and crows' feet permanently imprinted
on the corners of my eyes,
each line like a rolodex
full of stories—
the good, the bad; the joy, the sad.
But dig a little deeper under the surface,
and you will find a little boy
who will always live inside the walls of this aging body,
a younger self who did not have the words,
did not have the voice or skills to navigate
the complex world he was born into.
Insecure and scared,
he always pushed his needs down
to take care of others,
frozen in fear from seeking the love he always wanted
until his light was nothing more
than one last smoldering ember
almost extinguished
beneath piles of ashes,
having almost given up on this life.
Now I walk down gravel roads with my husband
side by side,
paying close attention
as we help one another heal,

comforting those two little boys
forever within us,
hand in hand—
growing older together,
finally finding our way home.

On C Block

Meagan and Sophi are transgender women who met and fell in love in a men's prison in California. While state law permits them to request a transfer to a women's facility, it does not guarantee that they would be moved together, so they have elected to remain where they are. I have been corresponding with them since 2020.

In the men's prison, San Diego,
Meagan and Sophi tell me they love
to feed the sparrows and the brown
rabbits that huddle
low in the grass.

If they sit so still
their own bodies forget them,
a rabbit brushes by like a sigh.

Sometimes Sophi runs and runs
miles round the track in her
taped-up shoes, watching the birds
skip the fence
and dart for the mountains.

At night, they open their tray slots
and reach out their arms.
Their fingers, dark with dirt,
can just touch.

Some Quiet Evenings

I go out to sit with them—thin
insects tuning their strings,
the night's first bat casting
in the breeze—and remember
that evening, hot and windless,
a new lover stripping
my bed, spreading my sheets
on the moonless grass.
Who were we then?
Young and swallowed
by the night. Unfinished.
Ill-matched.
Sirius trudged across
my narrow field of sky,
the whole universe sliding
away, a little more life
slipping out of me, again
so briefly in love.
Some quiet evenings I go out
to sit with them, all the men
I've been, and beneath
that same quilt of stars retrace
my path, the weak orbit
of every man to touch me.

There Should Be Flowers

There should be more to life
than disruption
and survival
but there isn't.
There should be birds
singing your name.
There should be paintings
the size of skyscrapers
memorializing your body.
There should be love
for you
in everything.
There should be a billion women
jumping at the same time
to move the earth off its course.
There should be parties
to celebrate
the end of this world.
There should be flowers
to welcome
a new one.

Apparition

I'm carrying an orange plastic bucket of compost
down from the top of the garden—sweet dark,

fibrous rot, promising—when the light changes
as if someone's flipped a switch that does

what? Reverses the day. Leaves chorusing,
dizzy. And then my mother says

—she's been gone more than thirty years,
not her voice, the voice of her in me—

You've got to forgive me. I'm choke and sputter
in the wild daylight, speechless to that:

maybe I'm really crazy now, but I believe
in the backwards morning I am my mother's son,

we are at last equally in love
with intoxication, I am unregenerate,

the trees are on fire, fifty-eight years of lost bells.
I drop my basket and stand struck

in the iron-mouth afternoon. She says
I never meant to harm you. Then

the young dog barks, down by the front gate,
he's probably gotten out, and she says,

calmly, clearly, *Go take care of your baby.*

My Father, My Hands

My father gave me these hands, fingers
inch-wide and muscular like his, the same
folds of skin like squinted eyes looking
back at me whenever I wash my hands
in the kitchen sink and remember him
washing garden dirt off his, or helping
my mother dry the dishes every night.

These are his fingernails—square, flat—
ten small mirrors I look into and see him
signing my report card, or mixing batter
for our pancakes on Sunday mornings.
His same whorls of hair near my wrists,
magnetic lines that pull me back to him
tying my shoelaces, pointing at words
as I learned to read, and years later:
greasy hands teaching me to change
the oil in my car, immaculate hands
showing me how to tie my necktie.

These are his knuckles—rising, falling
like hills between my veins—his veins,
his pulse at my wrist under the watch
he left for me ticking since his death,

alive when I hold another man's hand
and remember mine around his thumb
through the carnival at Tamiami Park,
how he lifted me up on his shoulders,
his hands wrapped around my ankles
keeping me steady above the world, still.

Father's Day

I'd like to be a father,
you said, your last week alive.
You'll make a great dad, I said.

Imagined the baby you might adopt,
who your partner might be,
and me, a grandfather.

Another Father's Day without you.
Without you,
I'm still your father.

You'll never accept me as a son,
you said, when you came out as trans.
You will always be my son.
You would have made a great dad.

DEAR SON

by Jason O'Toole

I never saved a Father's Day card from you, nor any other card. I'm not the kind to save cards, but I had thought I'd get plenty more in the years ahead. We had three years in which you didn't wish me a happy Father's Day or a merry Christmas, or say, "I forgive you." I could hardly expect you to say those words.

We spoke twice during that time, and it ended in tears for both of us. I'd call or text and you wouldn't answer. Not until I texted the words you were waiting to hear. Yes, I knew you for many years as my daughter, but of course I'd accept you as my son.

We reunited, and for a time, I was once again a real dad to you. I was there for your top surgery. I tried to help with your testosterone injection but got squeamish. Then a blood cancer stole our time with one another. I wish it was me instead who had died that night. There will never be another Father's Day card or call from you. I'll have to make do with the last "I love you" you spoke to me before I got you into the ambulance.

Because you are no longer here, I'll fight for your causes: trans rights, gay rights, economic, racial, and environmental justice. You taught me how to care again and demonstrated true courage. How, then, can I be a coward? What greater horror can the world show me than losing you? What can man's willful stupidity, arrogance, and laughable attempts at intimidation do when we know that love cannot be destroyed? The body can be broken, but never our bonds.

Rest now, my beloved son. Dad knows what to do.

Telling My Father

I found him on the porch that morning,
sipping cold coffee, watching a crow
dip down from the power line, into the pile
of black bags stuffed in the dumpster
where he pecked and snagged a can tab,
then carried it off, clamped in his beak
like the key to a room only he knew about.
My father turned to me then, taking in
the reek of my smoke, traces of last night's
eyeliner I decided not to wipe off this time.
Out late was all he said. And then smiled,
rubbing the small of my back through the robe
for a while, before heading inside, letting
the storm door click softly shut behind him.
Later, when I stepped into the kitchen again,
I saw it waiting there on the table: a glass
of orange juice he had poured for me and left
sweating in a patch of sunlight so bright
I couldn't touch it at first.

DiAnna

The day after my father died,
I was a balloon released
to the sky, nothing held me,
and I floated aimlessly in
the dark, eyes closed—

and then your voice came
to me, morning sun, warm
and bright. Brought bagels
in bed, climbed in beside me,
shared blankets, held me
and cried with me, steadied my
string. I took my first breath.

Still, even when wind comes,
you have me tied to your wrist—
you give me a little tug
to say: I am here, you are safe,

I have you.

Evidence

Down a wooded path
in dark, we board
glass-bottom canoes,

moon pregnant &
milkless. Step into
the boat, unsteady

in the shallows, listen
to night's canopy—
a hum of creatures

we can't see. Afloat,
we trail slim fingers
behind our bodies,

carve cerulean stripes
into the water, a fleet
of fireflies beneath

our seat, buoyant
& boundless. Science
says bioluminescence,

except I know of God
and how she planted
kinesthetic stars

within the bay, bright
sparks flowering.

Sun Star

For ES

After churning all night
I wake to see the sun star
In the window, its perfect
Blossoms full of light.
I smell coffee and hear you
Moving room to room.
In two weeks, we'll transplant
Our sun star to the front bed
Between the extravagant
Dragon flower and the delicate
Hyacinth which Homer says
Sprang from the blood of a boy
Killed by Zephyr, god of wind.
We'll root the flower well.
White threads of mycelia
Will embrace the tendrils,
Welcoming and nourishing
As we gradually inhabit
Our lives, every morning
Fiercely in love with light

Quantum Love

I wish you understood
what my love meant.
How it never was a particle
or a wave, but somehow
both at once.

Once created it could never be
destroyed, only transformed.

I've lit up cities with it since
you disappeared.
Wrote your name
in colored lights on skyscrapers
so the birds
might tell you where I am.

So the stars might
whisper in your ear
that yours is still the only
face I see when I close my
eyes against the setting sun.

In the Beginning

There was love. And out of love
came graves and mountains,
clefts in rocks, footsteps in gardens,
warm-blooded creatures
taking shape in darkness,
peppermills and grocery lists,
squirrels scrabbling on copper roofs,
the smalls of backs, the backs of necks,
tea lights and tapers,
badly sewn curtains,
sobs in the night, policemen on lawns,
IVs and ambulances,
skies full of stars
waiting for eyes
to see them as constellations.

A Reminder from the Stars

Constellations of stars exploded
to bring you to life.

The molecules in your left collarbone
come from a different galaxy than your right.

And by defiantly existing against all odds,
you are honoring their sacrifice.

Body Image

No matter how they

try to claim you, your body

can never belong to them. It will

always be ours. Piece by piece

I made you whole with my love,

shaped you to share with

the world. I gave you unbroken,

portion of my portion. This body, your

sacred text and map back to me.

However you fall, fail,

submit to frailty, your body

cannot conceal the message. My love,

you are the message.

Dearest Child

Let go and fly free—
Release to the wind
what is not truly you.
Embrace your essence
without damning inhibition.

Don't hold back for fear
of those who despise rainbows
and stardust, and the magic
of who you have always been.
They cower at your worth.

Hold my gaze, precious one—
Accept cozy warm respite,
celebration of your presence
in our fold of sparkling possibilities,
and delight that you have arrived.

Prayer for Werewolves

Someone will probably love you for who you are.
    If not, you'll still find friends,
friends who, given time, or given warning,
    will probably gather around you, hold your hands,
and wrap you in soft coats and blankets till the violence
    inside your body ends.

Someone will probably love you for who you are,
    not just for who you labor to be.
Maybe you're lost in your skin today. Maybe you're burning
    and wish you could tear it all off. Please don't. You are variously
a marvel, an athlete, a wilderness, a source of warmth
    and a way to learn from fear.

When you have claws, your claws are yours, your ears
    bristle and are yours; your irises
are citrine, pure, and yours. They let you see
    through smog and pine thickets and into the future, where
you need no chains to feel secure,
    and someone will probably love you for who you are:
then you will know each other's scents
    and nuzzle or lope together. But for
now, you have friends,
    who are not going anywhere. Please
stay here.

Watching My Friend Pretend Her Heart Isn't Breaking

On Earth, just a teaspoon of neutron star
would weigh six billion tons. Six billion tons
is equivalent to the weight of every animal
on earth, including insects. Times three.

Six billion tons sounds impossible
until I consider how it is to swallow grief—
just one teaspoon and one may as well have consumed
a neutron star. How dense it is,
how it carries inside it the memory of collapse.
How difficult it is to move then.
How impossible to believe anything
could ever lift that weight.

There are many reasons to treat each other
with great tenderness. One is
the sheer miracle we are here together
on a planet surrounded by dying stars.
One is we cannot see
what anyone else has swallowed.

I Need a Poem

Can we talk about the moon
tonight? Low & full
in the baby-blue sky. A friend
at my door, the sound
of her laugh & well-loved
heart. I want to be held
up like that. I need a poem
about happiness I haven't
written yet, an ode
to the ducks in my neighbours'
pool, another for the pink
magnolias of spring—some trees
make it look so easy: Yes,
I can hold all this beauty up.

Wedding Cathedral

Something about the light beneath those trees
transformed that lawn to a green cathedral.
The first time I entered, alone, the world grew still
and dust motes floated in the sun.

Today the tents are up and music's moving
on the air. A hundred chairs await their guests.
You're putting on your wedding dress,
bouquet of pinks and blues and yellows.

When I see a flower in your hair,
I hear that San Francisco song I used to play
when I was young and dreamed of kissing girls
with flowers in their hair.

My cousin starts the processional song.
Your sister turns and smiles at us.
You lift your shoulders in a happy shrug.
I feel the trees exhaling.

I Wish I Could Hug Her

My beloved sycamore succumbed to the storm—
her trunk cleaved, canopy splintered.
How she laid herself down

with such care. She spared me
from a caved-in roof and a crashing-
through the window to where

all my poems slept, tucked
behind their glass blanket. How
lucky I was, to have spent

a season-ago-day swimming
in her shade, where barefoot toes
tingled in the coolness

of her grassy skirt, and I day-
dreamed under her verdant
light-lace. Giddy in the embrace

of her branches—leafy-sleeved arms
foxtrotting upon a breeze, I could
feel a few dipping to graze my cheek

like a barely-there kiss
and a whisper—*I'm here.*
And how that was all I needed

to breathe.

White Oak

Before us, before we
covered this hill with flowers,
the forest kept the ground in place.
Now we coax from the dirt our food,
the little we can make grow.
We thank god for the shade
as we sweat through the day
and pray every storm
that the limbs above home
don't crash through.
The adjuster has little hope,
doesn't care how we fell in love
with a tree and chose it to build
our lives around. Neighbors whisper
we have a widowmaker
on our hands as if our family
isn't tethered already to tombstones,
as if we weren't once a forest.

Weekend Eternity

Saturday, my love
in sunlight tends the lawn.
A locust tree knits lace
from its own shadow, and I wish
I could cast a similar silhouette.

I fret over the honey-sweet
scent, the cluster and fall
of feathery blossoms, thorns
along those branches
where birds keen the day.

I pray the heartbroken
are blessed by fresh-cut grass,
pungent wild onions,
the petrichor of distant rain.
Right now, a faraway storm

rushes downriver. I think
I know what it runs from.
My love wipes his brow, bows to earth
beneath the locust, looks back
where he knows I will always be.

The Peace Lily

is a flower that can
grow and survive
even if it's left
in the shade.

See?

We don't always
choose our environment,

but we can't let that
stop us from blooming.

HOW TO TALK ABOUT IT, 2016

by Patrick Ramsay

Let me preface this by telling you I'm a pretty quiet person. There are a few reasons why, but mainly, being quiet is easy. You just sit back and witness. It's comfortable for me—or it was.

On June 12, 2016, I half-woke up in the middle of the night to reports in the media of a world trembling. Hoping it was a nightmare, I fell back into a restless sleep and woke up later that morning to a higher death toll. The world is crying now. I'm part of that world. It shakes, and I shake with it. I could hear my own pulse that morning. Pulse. Pulse. Pulse. I close my eyes and try to hear my friends' pulses too. There are 49 fewer pulses. In a group text message with my best friends, we say how much we love each other. The world is still crying. We don't know how to talk about it, but we learn their names. It's important that we know them. I don't know how to respond.

I break up with my boyfriend that night because all I can think about is how he implied that one reason he liked me was that he couldn't tell I was gay. How when I told him I was getting a yoga membership, he said that was "too gay." How I, a quiet person already, was consciously speaking less. And when I did speak, it was deeper. Mimicking the bro-talk of a macho asshole. The world is still crying, and I'd spent the past few months—maybe even the past years—trying to turn someone on with strategic linguistics. How messed up is that, man? I knew now how to respond.

I thought about all the times I was told to be quiet. I thought about terror telling love in Orlando to be quiet. And the word that kept coming back to me was *louder*. I need to be louder. Louder for my friends. Made family

by our trials. Louder for the time my sister said, *They should be able to get married, but they shouldn't be able to call it marriage.* Louder for the time my father scoffed and rolled his eyes at the headband I was wearing to hold back my long and swooping hair. I thought it was beautiful, but I cut it a few days later. Louder for the parts of myself I'm still afraid of. Louder for the hairy-legged man in a tight, sequined dress. I stare at him in the elevator because butterflies are rare in beehives.

Louder because it felt so good to walk down 25th Street proud to be holding a hand as big as mine while we hopped over sidewalk cracks and nearly danced through every crosswalk. That was a good day. Louder because his mother needs to know that even though I don't have the body to feed her grandchild or to fill a dress, I could find room on my hip for the child of her son and real space in my heart to love them no less.

Louder because the leading cause of death among Utah children ages 10 to 17 is suicide. Louder because there's a reason for that. Louder because 600 children. The world is still crying. Louder because the chief medical examiner of Utah says, *We're certainly on track for being over 600 this year.*

Because we're talking numbers now, think about it this way: The collective empty seats could fill 29 classrooms. Now, imagine walking through an empty school. Louder for the seventh grader who packaged every word in masculinity before it fell out of his mouth. Louder for the kid who is in bed at night not sleeping but begging God to make him straight.

Let me tell you a secret, sweet child: The power of prayer won't fix what isn't broken. I wish someone had told me that. Louder because I kept the real me so folded up and hidden away that even though I'm here now, I'm still trying to iron out the wrinkles. Louder because love isn't meant to be silenced. Louder because people aren't meant to be silenced.

Groundwork

A friend returned from Japan and described
how when new plants are to be added
to a garden, care is taken to both
nurture the new addition
and protect the existing
interconnected life around it.
Nemawashi, it is called, sometimes translated
as laying the groundwork, but really much more
intricate. Each root lovingly unearthed,
seen bare, its needs and direction revealed,
then a plan formed that includes its well-being,
avoiding amputations by spade,
starvation and thirst from
heedless prioritizing of the new shrub,
or erosion when the soil itself is no longer
held together.
Let me live, each one says,
and the gardener answers:
I want more than that for you.

Thirst

My love leaves little bits of greenery around the house,
she names them like she names all things she loves.
She does not ask me to water them.
She names me *darling,* as if I too had roots.

I do not interfere; I simply watch in awe.
Learning to hold life in her hands, like the mother
she never wanted to be. Perhaps she thinks that,
by virtue of this practice, she will know how to keep me watered.
Perhaps, in her way, she is learning to keep things from dying.

I said so many times that she doesn't need to keep me green,
but she is becoming a master all the same, prepared for my droughts.
What I meant to do was thank her,
what I meant to do was say I am so grateful for the water.

Naiad

Those years when my love
was a water nymph, swimming

mornings, weekends, on her lunch
break, at Portage Park, the Y, or

the university, her skin and hair
faintly fragranced with chlorine—

her signature scent. For some,
it's chocolate or oysters or

maybe figs. But give me
a whiff from a bottle of Clorox,

with its clean aroma, wholesome
as sheets flapping on a line

under a summer sun, and I'll be
drowning in thoughts of love.

Laundry

Between the two of us, it's me
who does the laundry. Alone
in the basement, I draw out
the trap, pulling the lint
from the screen. Its gray surface
tears, tender between my fingers.
Flecks of paper. An eyelash.
A dog whisker. I find fibers
from your red sweatshirt,
my pink bra, the yellow underwear
you picked up on our honeymoon.
This muted fluff collects
your smell, holds your skin.
We call what I am doing a chore.
The machine cycles from wet
to dry, turning over another winter,
another summer, another year.
Kneeling before the dryer door,
a dim light from a bare bulb overhead,
I have everything I've ever wanted.

So Much Happiness

It is difficult to know what to do with so much happiness.
With sadness there is something to rub against,
a wound to tend with lotion and cloth.
When the world falls in around you, you have pieces to pick up,
something to hold in your hands, like ticket stubs or change.
But happiness floats.
It doesn't need you to hold it down.
It doesn't need anything.
Happiness lands on the roof of the next house, singing,
and disappears when it wants to.
You are happy either way.
Even the fact that you once lived in a peaceful tree house
and now live over a quarry of noise and dust
cannot make you unhappy.
Everything has a life of its own,
it too could wake up filled with possibilities
of coffee cake and ripe peaches,
and love even the floor which needs to be swept,
the soiled linens and scratched records . . .
Since there is no place large enough
to contain so much happiness,
you shrug, you raise your hands, and it flows out of you
into everything you touch. You are not responsible.
You take no credit, as the night sky takes no credit
for the moon, but continues to hold it, and share it,
and in that way, be known.

More

The mist that covers our mountain
Evaporates and becomes a feeling
That lasts all morning. You lift the spoon
From the sauce and feel the texture
Of the aroma. I love the way
You say silly things pretending
To be serious, the way you lift
The spoon almost touching your lips.
Steam rises from the pot.
Mist rises from the mountain.
All things rise, merge, divide
And merge again. We're old
And I want more of what we have.
Nothing different, just more.
Not forever. Just a few more years.
It's taken so long to arrive.

Worship

Sunday comes, and it is always
a miracle. Not because of god,
but because there is nothing
we believe in except our ability
to get by, together. Is it not a miracle
we made it through another week
happy? The pantry stocked
with fruit leather, words at our throat
a sticky gift, the light at the window
a forehead kiss. And you by my side
folding school uniforms, running a bath,
holding us together hour by hour.
Divorce me from anything holy
that is not here, for this is my religion.

ANNA LUCIA DELOIA

My Favorite Love Poems

are concerned with ordinary things:
yellow tomatoes, like your mom grows
on the porch in summer, your focaccia
before it goes into the oven—all raw
flour and oil, the soapy, sea salt smell
of our hands, rinsing off afternoon
light in the kitchen sink. Precise enough
to be unknowable, they still begin
in me a slow, deep swelling,
an insistent voice announcing:
this has been our life.
Yes. My favorite love poems are about
(whatever else they are about)
you
and the way you tear open my days
like still-warm bread.

Anniversary

It didn't happen like in the movies.
There were no balloons or red cards with hearts,
no fancy plated dinner or spectacular overtures
to testify our love. We sat at the kitchen table
with handwritten notes from our journals.
I cut the perforated edge, his ripped like any other
letter on any other day. We did the same old thing—
mused on the stories that hold our lives together,
how we met that fateful day, the time we ran through
a slot canyon, all the family dinners and how perfectly
my head fits into his chest, my body into his.
"Three years, huh?" he said. "Yeah, habibi, three years," I said.
Some want loud announcements and celebrations,
some measure love by the price tag, others by surprise.
All I want is what I already have. The millions of quiet gestures
that together compose a symphony of care.
His hand in mine, soft jazz, fresh-baked banana bread,
the way he asks about my day, and listens.

Recuerdo

Let me take it through my heart again,
that unchanging moment,
you wading through the river,
me wading toward you, laughing,
the illumination of that moment,
the shine of our skin
and clouds coming toward us.
They are the sky beings who live above
with tears ready to fall
like the origins of rain; no one knows
what they have seen in their previous fluid form.

For now, I merely go through that one day again,
remembering, traveling toward the river
past the place where snakes shed their skin
against stone
and move on
new, shining like a constant,
ceaseless stream of water
as it crawls across earth, changes and passes
blood memory, saltwater memory,
toward our laughter and joy
that moves once again through this heart.

Patchwork

For Ellie, Avery, and Adriel

It's 1 a.m. and the sound of laughter
rolls down the steps and flows
under the door of my bedroom.
Upstairs, my daughter and her
girlfriend, here for spring break,
and her older sister are snuggled
on the couch, laughing. Three
different tones and timbres,
giggle, chuckle, chortle, all
harmonizing like a song.
Their happiness covers me
like a quilt, a contact joy that
stitches warmth and light
into this dark night.

Milkweed

For my daughter

My thoughts try to catch up with your telling.
Already three months into hormone therapy?
Black-eyed Susans in bloom,
the maples are starting to turn.

How did I miss this?
Your softening features,
smooth skin, and coy smile

change like the season in front of me.

I see milkweed pods
split wide open,
birthing perfect rows of seed,
secrets given away, one at a time.

Each brown beginning
broken free on the breeze,
with hair grown soft, so very soft,
while change is on the wind.

Summering in Wildwood, NJ

in a few days, i'll be on a beach
so bright i can see the sun through my fingers,

each thin vein lit
up blue like a heron's leg.

this poem is not so much about a beach
as it is about arriving,

blowing stop signs
until the coast affirms

that lines are always changing,
and the tide tells me

my body can morph
as many times as it needs.

Time Travel

I see her in every young girl
With a certain haircut.
She has been pushed
Aside to make way for
Me. And yet she is me.
I always believed in time travel.
The idea of seeing
Yourself, and guiding you on
Your way. I don't grieve the woman
I could have become,
But it is the truth:
I would do anything
To protect that little girl
I once was. I like to
Imagine her in the laughs
Of every youth, and I
See her structure
In the build of my character.
I always believed in time travel.
Yet there's not a thing I
Would change, as she
Became me.

How I wanted to be beautiful

Leaping with arms raised
to save a goal.
Standing firm and tall
at first base.
Moving a cleat through
the red infield dirt.
Pressing the spiked sole into
soft soil and seeing
divots look back at me.
Proof I could make a mark.

I didn't want to be a boy
but I wanted to be
treated like one.
Bolt of thunder
free from hairclips,
dresses and dolls.
Pride for what I did
and not how I looked.

I didn't feel like a girl either.
I felt like one of the murky-rooted
cottonwoods at the edge of the creek,
a lake shining in sunrise,
air just above an oak at the crest of a hill.

Shimmering, I pulled up my roots
every morning. Put on t-shirts
and went to school where I
prismed into a thousand veins of light.

Later came the trying to fit in.
Slicked-back hair and
low cut shirts. Wanting to be
beautiful and chosen.

But early on I knew the best
beauty came among
trees and green rivers
and no need to be
perceived as anything
but a body among bodies,
no thought towards
what I wore or who saw.

A SELF DISCOVERED, A SELF CREATED

by Andrés Larios Brown

My two brown eyes: sisters, not twins. I hold my breath as I try to match the winged eyeliner of my left eye to my right eye. The slightest flick can make the difference, a skill never intended to be mastered by a person like me. I exhale with my success—a sacred *amen* before I add the final step. Mascara elongating my eyelashes and highlighting what all the women at church would always compliment me on. If only they could see me now, in my self-bestowed rite and ritual of congruence. The forbidden fruit of femininity. If only they could've seen me *then*—though being visible and being seen don't always mean the same thing.

My mom didn't teach me how to be a beautiful son, though she did pass her hair down to me—defiant curls as unruly as her spirit. The coarseness comes from my dad—I'm told that's needed in order to survive as an immigrant. My hair is a beautiful mixture, *una mezcla bella*—both colonizer and colonized. I blow it out every three days. A sacrament of products and processes. Heat and pressure help smooth out the curls and give it a beautiful shine, though this also weakens the strands. Both Samson and Delilah, I run my fingers through my miraculously long hair, anointing my head with argan oil for strength and beauty. Maybe someday I'll embrace my natural curls, reclaim them for myself and my ancestors. Find new rituals of worship.

My reflection feels like scripture for me—I study it daily with devotion. A radical practice in a world that taught me shame. My they/them: a hymn of queer celebration, a sermon of freedom and self-love. Not a wrestle between either/or, but the peace of both/and. Unshackled by limits, I rejoice: *Halleluiah! Glory to me, in the highest!* Resilient, I rest in a profound gratitude for all that makes me *me*. I am the fullness of my own creation. Not an act of a western god, but a pilgrimage back to self—reclaiming my holy land, *mi tierra sagrada*.

The World Loves You Back

Even if no one ever touched you
with the tenderness you needed,
believe that the world's been
holding you in its arms since
the day you were born. You are
not an accident, or afterthought.
Let rain on the roof remind you.
Let sun on the skin, and the neon-
orange of the Mexican sunflower
at which a hummingbird pauses
to drink. There are so many ways
to hold and be held, and you
could spend your whole life
tallying them up without ever
reaching the end of the list.

Heart Rock

On the bank of the Trinity River
I find a heart-shaped rock,
perfectly smooth
with a big scar in the center.
I used to fill my pockets with treasure:
pebbles, shells, bones and bark.
Now I just hold each one
and put it back where
it came from, a prayer
to remain in place.
But this worn stone,
with its distinct injury slightly
shining in the sun, comes home
with me. It sits in the center
of my altar, and I coddle it
every morning. I cup it gently
and it exists as an unruined symbol
of ongoing work, the might
of mending that is left
in my hands alone.

Mending

I recently took up mending—
that simple task of renewal.
It's harder than it seems
to put something back together again.
The ragged hole
somehow larger than the cloth left to cover it,
and yet I am drawn to
this tangible act of repair—
the precise puncture point of the needle
making a new hole to fix the old,
the supple sound of thread drawing through fabric,
and then the repetition
prick, thread, prick, thread—
the mending a meditation
the meditation a mending.

I don't know if I'm drawn to this
because the world has so many frayed edges
and I have only needle and thread
and my words to weave it back together.

Or perhaps it's simply the best way
I know how to make things whole,
my head bent over

the ripped knees of my son's jeans,
each stitch
both a patch and a prayer
to keep him safe
to keep us whole
to repair the world.

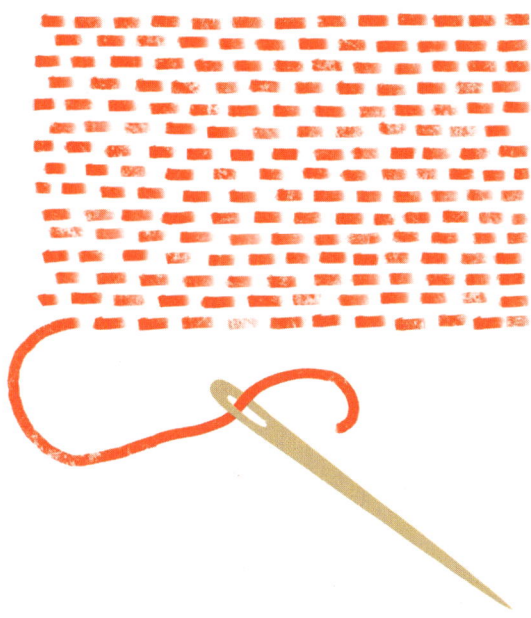

Missives

What do the hummingbirds know
of my breaking? Still as knots
on bare branches, they perch
above my COVID sleep. Sprites
or messengers. When last I grieved
an untimely death—a shrinking world,
the buzz of their wings soothed
in wordless song my sorrow. They pip
flutter, hover inches from my face—
like a question I haven't answered.
Three grams of mysterious, with swift
needle tongues. These nectar seekers
come bearing lessons about tenacity—
voices tiny with whispered promises.

At Chautauqua Lake with My Granddaughter

Each morning she refills my bird-feeders, films
the orioles' return from the kitchen window.

Yesterday she spied a hawk. Her face rapt, she traced
its wide-spread wings sweeping across the broad sky.

Weeding the garden, she cradled a worm in soil-stained hands,
called it by name, gently returned it to earth.

On this clear May night, we lie on cool grass,
awed by the Milky Way's scattered scroll.

Tilting her chin upward, she says she wants to go there,
her mouth full of questions—

How big is the universe? Are there others?
Is there life out there?

Our bodies warm against each other, I have no answers.
I hold her tight, pray her heart stays open against the dark.

Abundance

My grandfather, with his bronzed hands
full of dark soil from planting dahlias,
tells me to focus on the bounty
we have been given:

A sky so wide and full
that it carries every color
of blue and pink and orange
you can imagine.

And a sun that warms us
from our head to our toes,
and gives us reason sometimes to say,
Beautiful weather today!

And a moon so gentle
that she even wins the stormy seas over
and gives us a beauty to gaze at
in the arms of our lovers.

And a planet of such abundance
that it gives us so much nourishment;
shade in the form of trees,
flowers that glow radiant for our eyes to see.

So do not despair at all your falls.
There is still happiness
to be had here,
no matter how small.

An example, my grandfather says,
while looking at my grandmother,
is that with just a good heart and some tenderness,
you, too, can have a love that lasts lifetimes.

Woodland You

It's easy to look at the contours of a forest and feel
a bone deep love for nature.
It's less easy to remember that the contours of your own body
represent the exact same nature.
The pathways of your mind.
Your dreams,
dark and strange as sprouts curling beneath a flat rock.
Your regret,
bitter as the citrus rot of old cut grass.
It's the same as the nature you make time to love.
That you practice loving.
The forest. The meadow. The sweeping arm of a galaxy.
You are as natural as any postcard landscape
and deserve the same love.

One Heart

Look at the birds. Even flying
is born

out of nothing. The first sky
is inside you, open

at either end of day.
The work of wings

was always freedom, fastening
one heart to every falling thing.

Heart to Heart

It's neither red
nor sweet.
It doesn't melt
or turn over,
break or harden,
so it can't feel
pain,
yearning,
regret.
It doesn't have
a tip to spin on,
it isn't even
shapely—
just a thick clutch
of muscle,
lopsided,
mute. Still,
I feel it inside
its cage sounding
a dull tattoo:
I want, I want—
but I can't open it:
there's no key.
I can't wear it
on my sleeve,

or tell you from
the bottom of it
how I feel. Here,
it's all yours, now—
but you'll have
to take me,
too.

DEAR DAUGHTER

by Annette Langlois Grunseth

The first time we heard your heartbeat, when I felt that first blip of a kick inside me, and then the day you were born, we marveled at the miracle of you. Curious and creative, you asked profound questions at age three as we sat on the grass watching clouds in a summer sky. You were awestruck by the stars at age eight, you and Dad on a blanket in the backyard looking up at the Milky Way. You even arranged glow-in-the-dark stars in accurate constellations on your bedroom ceiling.

We worried about you at age nine when the anxiety began. We sought help. Counselors and doctors tried, yet you struggled. You finished high school and college with honors. You married your soulmate right after college. Still, anxiety and depression followed you like a shadow. You said you felt separate from the whole world and from your sense of self, withdrawing and feeling worse as the years passed.

One September afternoon as we gathered in the family room, you asked Dad and me to read a letter you spent months writing. I noticed your hair was longer on top, getting curly. We read silently as you watched us. *This has been a long time coming. I identify as a woman.* We felt a bolt of awareness surge through us. Of course! Thinking back over those anxious years, how did we miss the signs?

In our surprised silence, you asked for a hug. We embraced you like we did our precious newborn, that eight-year-old starstruck kid, that unsure teen: now on this day in the family room, a relieved daughter. You helped us learn the language of gender identity and dysphoria. You were patient with us as we practiced using she/her pronouns. Later, I asked, *How did you know you were a woman?*

You turned the question back to me. *Mom, how did you know you were a woman?*

I just knew.

Me too! you answered.

Since your transition, you have flourished with confidence and joy. Still awestruck by stars and the universe, you work with astronomers around the world practicing astrophotography. You discovered how to love yourself while you and your spouse have been married, now more than 20 years. Our love for you is as big as the universe—infinite and boundless—and we are thankful for the woman you've become.

Heart

She has painted her lips
hibiscus pink.
The upper lip dips
perfectly in the center

like a Valentine heart.
It makes sense to me—
that the lips, the open

ah of the mouth
is shaped more like a heart
than the actual human heart.
I remember the first time I saw it—

veined and shiny
as the ooze of a snail—
if this were what
we had been taught to draw

how differently we might have
learned to love.

Be Mine

We valentined our way through February
and at the center pulsed my holiday
birthday: red hearts, red cake, red letters
everywhere, a love-massacre with red balloons
hovering under our low vaulted ceilings.

Don't buy red roses on Valentine's Day
I told my ex-husband. They're hothouse
and overpriced. What about a nice houseplant?
Maybe a pothos—Devil's ivy—leaves splay
wide like open palms. They're hard to kill.
And skip the candy boxes, with their heart-
shape and all their cream-filled randomness.

For many years, I have been my own valentine—
treated myself like a special occasion,
I'd buy my own candy and flowers,
accept the handmade cards of my children
scrawled in crayon and call it enough.

This morning I hear the snowplow's scrape.
Soon I will join my neighbors clearing
the driveway and sidewalk, lifting my back
to the industry of snow. I am grounded
to love—feeling it, being in it,
even as I windmill the shovel above my head,
letting the crystals fall into my face.

Pockets of Joy

Cleaning out old clothes from childhood,
I came across a pair of worn-out camouflaged jeans
I once had to be bribed to get out of.
Holding them in my hands sparked flashes of days
spent under the canopies of trees on fire with color
back when I took the time to savor chasing falling leaves,
relishing in the excitement
each time I caught one in my outstretched hands
depositing them in my pants as if they were a treasure
to be withdrawn at some later date.
Perhaps it was a premonition
for this moment when life feels less simple,
and we all need to reach into our pockets of joy,
pulling out golden shards of oak and maple leaves
stowed away from all those years ago,
until it is finally time to cash them in
for that precious memory of happier days
we thought we had forgotten.

My Love

A lone remaining leaf
trembles in the early air
like the one soft memory
of how we met so many
years ago. In the midst
of all the noise and traffic,
something very simple and
ancient trembled between
us like this leaf. And every
worry and plan fell away.
From that moment, I only
wanted to be near you, the
way a hummingbird does
all that work to simply
hover near something
sweet and lasting.

The Something

Time to notice drops of dew
on every fallen leaf, to draw a finger
through the tiny pools of light,

to watch a body's shadow
casting backward on the leaves,
to feel the sun's surprising heat,

this late October day.
Time to feel the veil of—something—
the *something* that exists

between me and her, invisibly pulling,
as I sit in sunlight waiting
for a single leaf to drop,

and catch it in mid-flight.
I can *feel* her texting—*please bring mushrooms,*
I want to make a soup for you.

I want to make you tea

What will come of these leaves?
Bright red as an elopement.
Thick-bodied rose hips hang heavy.
Tell me about your dreams again—
the one with yellow-sheened air,
the one where your lungs became sky.
Sit with me under the plum tree
and trace our lifelines together—
how they branch, how they wing.

Ginger Tea

in the summertime I don't think to make tea in the morning
in the winter I wake up, put the kettle on almost immediately,
without thinking

it is winter now and
I am still drinking you in like tea keeping me warm all day long

mug after mug it is your mug making my mind all muddled—
I am reusing the same ginger stem until the strands fall apart

today when I could do nothing
I tried to do everything but drink you in,
fearful of reaching the last drop

Winter Becomes Us

At the end of a gloomy week spent
huddled under piles of blankets
sipping cinnamon tea to stay warm
my wife and I woke before dawn
to offer winter a proper greeting.

Our lungs full of aliveness,
we exhale tiny clouds of ice
as crisp snow crunches underfoot
sending a wakeup call
through the sleeping woods.

We are the sole humans to traverse
this trail since the fresh snowfall,
two pairs of boot prints
perfectly pressed alongside
a lone set of coyote tracks.

Morning dawns under our watch
the sky burning slowly
from pink to bluebird
as light filters in around us
and her eyes blaze a fire inside.

Tentative Grace

Forgive me for hiding inside of me the small log cabin
with pungent herbs hanging from the rafters,
the sunlight that falls across the wood floor,
the wise woman pouring tea at the table.

Forgive me for squirreling away the animals of my forest.
The mountain lion watching absolutely everything,
the deer living in such tentative grace, always ready to spring.
The bear rumbling past in search of berries.

Forgive me for keeping myself so safe that I won't even
show you the wonders here—the crystal clusters glinting.
The magic so palpable, it moves along the skin of your arm like electricity.
Forgive me for matching the wallpaper so perfectly, my chameleon skin
peeling as if I am nothing more than the wall of an empty house.

Forgive me too for not being able to do the impossible, to transmute
the poisons of the lineage into something sweet. I have tried.
I have taken in so much that it nearly killed me. Forgive me for not dying,
for staying. For trying to become visible again. Forgive me now if I show up,
show myself. Forgive me if I become resplendent, if I smell of
pine needles and dirt, if I sound like the water in a stream skipping over rocks.
If I walk up the trail toward you and I say, "Can you see me?"

Ask Me Later

What is the difference between trees and clouds
when my present is the past to my future. This
seeing that I am turns the world as round as any
star and as round as the space stars hang in. If
you close your eyes you will find me resting my
head on the garden of your chest. If you ask me
anything I will answer truthfully. Then I will become

the object of your dreams the way you have been
the object of mine. Walking around I look for you.
Sitting I feel so embarrassed and my face feels
flushed. You are unaware of the effect you have
on me despite my vastness. I suppose it makes
sense to be both complete and completely lost as
you do your thing while stars do what they do too.

For Us

I was lost
under what they said about me.
I wore all their words,
weighing more than my bones,
carrying them everywhere I went.
I couldn't find myself
beneath those dirty fingerprints.
It was not me I saw
in the mirror, but I found
myself for you, for me, for us.
I pierced through the sun
to burn it all and to
come to you as I am.
We'll meet under the moon
while the night clouds
float through my hair.
I'll hold your hand
and nothing will weigh me down
while I fly in your love.

Twenty-One Love Poems [Poem III]

Since we're not young, weeks have to do time
for years of missing each other. Yet only this odd warp
in time tells me we're not young.
Did I ever walk the morning streets at twenty,
my limbs streaming with a purer joy?
did I lean from any window over the city
listening for the future
as I listen here with nerves tuned for your ring?
And you, you move toward me with the same tempo.
Your eyes are everlasting, the green spark
of the blue-eyed grass of early summer,
the green-blue wild cress washed by the spring.
At twenty, yes: we thought we'd live forever.
At forty-five, I want to know even our limits.
I touch you knowing we weren't born tomorrow,
and somehow, each of us will help the other live,
and somewhere, each of us must help the other die.

Earnestly, I Ask

Wait, don't go.
I don't care that there are 27,
sometimes 28, years between us, my love,
our time together has been timeless,
our sixteen years loving
need at least sixteen more, please
don't go.

Please wait somehow
for me to age beside your aging,
for my hair to whiten
and grey against the day beside your grey,
for my face to welcome lines of time
the way your beautiful face has
sketched the hours
upon the corners of your eyes,
your cheeks and mouth,
your forehead, darling, wait for me—

I am still a fledgling elder
in your shadow
of wisdom
and flight,
a horizon lies on your hipbones
and my head is in your lap
asking
no begging,
please
wait, don't go.

Past Perfect

Northampton, 2022

I lean on your shoulder
the evening light I love
fading from trunk to trunk

✦

Almost full
moon spills
across your dreaming face

✦

I close my eyes
and there you are
a summer that isn't ending

✦

It's all right you murmur
and I believe you
even though you're talking in your sleep

Neighbors

My husband and I are houses.
Neighbors when we lie down

at night, pillows like snow-filled yards.
Even if we touch walls, kiss

one windowsill to another, still
there is glass and brick between us.

I study the architecture of their face
as they dream. Blinds drawn,

memories on like evening news.
Childhood scenes? Today replayed?

I can't tell from here.
This is how we live in marriage.

Wandering alone the blue dawn
I lock and unlock doors,

some I've never opened to anyone,
closets cluttered with darkness.

What are you thinking about?
they ask, now awake. I glance up

from my pile of loose thoughts,
fold a few away before I answer,

the way people straighten a room
before letting someone in.

Far North

Spring rolls in hard—swift, brash, heedless.
Box elder saplings, blackberry and burdock
break ground any place we leave alone.

A dozen dark purple tulips sprang up
by the front steps. Did we plant them?
Another gesture I can't remember—

what I conceived, things I once said
with such conviction. How I got from there
to here. I am not the person

who moved here from Pittsburgh decades ago,
but I feel her inside me—
earnest, righteous, drowning in want.

I find a broken blue egg in front of our house
and I want to ask my wife if she believes
it is an omen of loss

or a beginning. Sometimes I find her
crying in the shower. I am struck by all
I can't take from her hands,

like the water running between them.

My Sexual Orientation Is Spring

We change time,
make the days longer.
I start to forget
the pact I made
with unhappiness,
take myself
to the ocean,
say *I just need*
to catch the last
few minutes
of light. This is
how spring is love,
the way it pulls us
towards pleasure.

Isn't Every Love Poem an Unfinished Love Poem?

Praise the ear.
Praise the hair curling
around the ear.

Praise the music
we never turn on,
only make.

Praise the caps
of your shoulders, my lips
pressed against them.

Praise the poem
I was trying to finish
when you showed up

at my door.

First Love

I don't think I ever really kissed
any boys. I think my tongue had
just been punching their tongues.

But as soon as you loved me
all my callous went away.
My hands so soft it hurt to pray.

You'd pick me up at my Catholic college
and I'd sleep for hours until we reached your house.
The first time in my life I'd ever rested,

the first time I didn't have to play a role
I'd never really wanted to get.
That's the medicine it is

to be finally seen by someone.

THE DOOR

by Justin Marsh

There was no telling how I would feel when I opened the door to greet them. They were a stranger, after all. Just someone I felt I knew so well because of constant texting for the week leading up to this moment. What was I doing? I didn't really know this person. Sure, I wasn't a novice when it came to internet hookups, but I usually treated them more like transactions. Instant gratification in the heat of a moment. But I felt like there was more to this person because I had already allowed myself to connect with them more deeply. This couldn't just be transactional. I couldn't let it be. I felt invested—even though, let's face it, I was also no stranger to getting way too deep, way too fast, into something totally unreachable.

I paced around the hotel room, downplaying the seriousness of what I was about to do. I'd done this sort of thing countless times. But I drank more then, burying my feelings of doubt and worth, altering my mind to a place where, if I was not met with the respect I deserved—a reciprocation of emotion—I would be able to move forward and simply blame it on the alcohol. Placate the voices in my head. Move on.

Distance and the holidays had prevented us from meeting up right away. It built a space, forcing us to converse about topics other than our primal desires. Maybe this would be different. After all, most of my experiences had been with cisgender (when one's gender identity matches the gender assigned at birth) men. This *was* going to be different. But I have no idea what I am doing. What if it's terrible? What if *I'm* terrible?

I checked my phone every three seconds for an update, until I was told they were on their way. Pure panic. No turning back now. Moments later—a knock. There was no telling how I would feel when I opened the door to greet them. A twist of the knob and there they were. Did I even say anything? Did they? I can't recall. I pulled them in for a kiss before the door had even closed behind them.

The next six hours were a blur. Time stood still, and yet somehow also warped at light speed. Finally, with some protest on my part, they had to return home, and soon enough they were gone. What I had just experienced was the safest I had felt in a long time. Completely untethered to reality and my usual inner dialogue. There was no awkward fumbling, no need to explain things, justifying my body or my appearance. My stretch marks against their surgery scars. My big, soft belly connecting with their tiny frame.

I lay there in disbelief. I wanted to just press repeat, like on a new song you can't get enough of, and play it over and over and over and over . . . replaying every moment I had just experienced in my mind. So this is what intimate human connections are all about? How was it possible that I had been gifted this experience? Had I just dreamt this entire thing?

Now, every time they leave, I'm instantly waiting for the next time they return with a soft knock at the door. But this time around, I know exactly how I'll feel—safe, loved, and unabashedly myself.

To Love a Woman

There is no kiss that I love more
than that of a woman. Yet, each woman
leaves too soon. About to create
our own way of touching, she admitted
to being too swept up in heartbreak
to make a story with my body.
Her soft mouth helped me
invent my definition of pleasure.
Her breath smelled sweet like carrots.
The idea was, we would speak
the same language and drive out
to the arroyo, never needing to return.
I don't know what will happen next.
She is a sacred text that I might
hold for years before finally
flipping a page. I could end up
an old woman in a black dress
standing at the counter
as the sun rises again with its orange
soak of light. And she could be
in the other room, asleep
with my cut braid
wrapped around her wrist.

Girl Crush

You gave me butterflies
and I tried hard to cut their wings
even though they came to me so naturally.

I'm so glad it didn't work.

Now we're watching them flutter about
from the kitchen window of our new house,
dancing and singing with our baby.

The source

For 天野

Early summer.
Under park trees
a Mourning Cloak butterfly
flickers an ellipse
over the sunlit patch of grass
where you are
reading, where I am watching
you read, then settles by you
like your notebook
—open, forgotten.

You are a statue with hair
a breeze runs fingers through,
still as a word
I could peer into for life.

The wind begins gently
to turn the leaves of your notebook up
onto your elbow: one, two,
a cadence—it's all unfolding
our future building against your arm.
It flutters but does not leave.

I vow to stare into the source with you—
hold it open—never look away.

Wings, thin as paper, shiver.
Stay.

Wings

A black and yellow striped
caterpillar chews a milkweed leaf,
spins a green-jewel chrysalis
with a smidge of gold,
cocoons until it transforms
into a butterfly with strong
wings that can fly far.

My daughter transitioned, too.
You may not understand
her biology, but like the Monarch,
she grew wings to fly,
to be herself. She's
the best cloud catcher I know.

Chrysalis

They told us this much: to wait
for chitin to split, for the emergence
of dazzling colors and pumping wings.

But they never talked about
what really happened inside:
how the caterpillar's whole body
dissolves,
how for a time
there is nothing but soupy liquid,
butterfly goo, formless but for the
rigid purse holding it in midair.

And no one told us, either,
that when the caterpillar was born,
while it grew and crawled along,
a few cells called *imaginal*
already held instructions for what to build
when it came time for another body.
Here, the shining eye, the scaled wings.

Let me remind you of the power
of sticking around.

If you feel shapeless and scared,
imagine yourself in that tiny,
thin-walled shell, whistling in the dark,
some part of you already knowing the way.

Emergence

Shackled by a cloak of expectations;
modesty and meekness
woven deep within the flesh.

Peel back layers of shame,
of fear and false facades.

A soul laid bare
in trauma and truth
can finally feel the sun.

The Facts of Life

That you were born
and you will die.

That you will sometimes love enough
and sometimes not.

That you will lie
if only to yourself.

That you will get tired.

That you will learn most from the situations
you did not choose.

That there will be some things that move you
more than you can say.

That you will live
that you must be loved.

That you will avoid questions most urgently in need of
your attention.

That you began as the fusion of a sperm and an egg
of two people who once were strangers
and may well still be.

That life isn't fair.
That life is sometimes good
and sometimes even better than good.

That life is often not so good.

That life is real
and if you can survive it, well,
survive it well
with love
and art
and meaning given
where meaning's scarce.

That you will learn to live with regret.
That you will learn to live with respect.

That the structures that constrict you
may not be permanently constricting.

That you will probably be okay.

That you must accept change
before you die
but you will die anyway.

So you might as well live
and you might as well love.
You might as well love.
You might as well love.

Instead of Depression

try calling it hibernation.
Imagine the darkness is a cave
in which you will be nurtured
by doing absolutely nothing.
Hibernating animals don't even dream.
It's okay if you can't imagine
spring. Sleep through the alarm
of the world. Name your hopelessness
a quiet hollow, a place you go
to heal, a den you dug,
Sweetheart, instead
of a grave.

Cento Between the Ending and the End

Sometimes you don't die
when you're supposed to
& now I have a choice
repair a world or build
a new one inside my body
a white door opens
into a place queerly brimming
gold light so velvet-gold
it is like the world
hasn't happened
when I call out
all my friends are there
everyone we love
is still alive gathered
at the lakeside
like constellations
my honeyed kin
honeyed light
beneath the sky
a garden blue stalks
white buds the moon's
marble glow the fire
distant & flickering
the body whole bright-
winged brimming
with the hours
of the day beautiful
nameless planet. Oh

friends, my friends—
bloom how you must, wild
until we are free.

NOW IS OUR TIME

I was 18 years old when, without my parents' knowledge, I voluntarily enlisted to serve my country. I remember that day vividly, as I couldn't have been prouder to be following in my grandfather's footsteps, a man I idolized and who also served in the Air Force. I grew up in a poor family, in a rural area in the southwest corner of Vermont. Like many young men and women in my community, college was not an option for me, and so I thought my greatest possibility for a higher education and brighter future would be through the military. My plan was to serve my time and utilize the benefits of the GI Bill, thus fulfilling two dreams: to serve my country and eventually graduate from college.

Off to basic training I went, where I was under no illusions about the difficult transition ahead. I remember how scared I was that first night, ushered off the plane in Texas, placed on a bus with other new recruits, riding in complete silence until we arrived on base. Then nothing but yelling, and picking up and putting down our bags until we moved in total unison as a team. I won't bore you with more details of training, but suffice it to say it was a period of rapid growth. In that short time, I gained confidence and purpose while connecting with my brothers and sisters from across the nation—every ethnicity, religion, and culture coming together to grow as a team and defend this country. I had proven I could make it on my own.

Directly after basic, I went to tech school for my Security Forces education. During this time, I began to change. What I had suppressed for so long began knocking on my soul. My service, my brotherhood, my bond to the people around me grew stronger—yet I couldn't confide in anyone, because if I did, everything I had worked so hard for would be taken away. I started feeling depressed.

I graduated from tech school, but before heading to Shaw Air Force Base for my first tour, I was granted 30 days of well-deserved leave. I was so proud to have earned my Security Forces badge and beret, and I remember arriving at the airport feeling three inches taller in my dress blues, with a sense of accomplishment I had never felt before. I was greeted at the airport with a hero's welcome from my entire family, and a huge sign that read, *Welcome home, Brad! We are so proud of you.* Back in Vermont, I felt like I was contributing to something larger for both my country and community.

When I arrived in South Carolina, however, things quickly deteriorated. I became further depressed, and most nights I couldn't sleep. I would wake up at one, two, three in the morning and go out to the track to run, sometimes for hours, just to suppress the pain. Here I was, surrounded by people who genuinely cared for me, in a stable environment for one of the first times in my life, and I had to hide who I was. I finally started seeing a therapist on base, and my life changed forever.

I came out as a gay soldier. The reaction was swift.
Because of the disastrous policy of "Don't Ask, Don't
Tell," I was released from the military for being gay,
though they labeled it an "antisocial personality disorder."
Discharged from the family I had created, simply for
being who I was, rejected and sent home, I felt like a
disgrace. After volunteering to serve, after raising my
right hand and swearing to defend, protect, and give my
life for this country, I was discriminated against by my
own government. There would be no GI Bill for me, no
support system; there would be no hero's welcome home
this time. Only lots of questions, concerns, lies, and
so much shame it almost made me pull the trigger and
end my life. How could I face my family, my friends, my
community as a failure? How many brave men, women,
and trans people have taken their lives because of the
shame our government has placed upon them simply for
being who they are?

Now, after decades of carrying around this pain, I am
speaking out to ensure no LGBTQIA+ person ends their
life because they feel rejected by our government or other
people. I will not sit idly by while books are banned and
policies are put into place that shame and limit people
for becoming themselves. I will not sit by to watch this
disgraceful, disqualifying discrimination happen again.
Lives are at stake.

Now is our time to stand strong and rise united, embracing
each other for all of our differences. Now is the time
to open our arms and strengthen our communities,

so that we all have a place to belong and call home, where we are celebrated and loved for exactly who we are. I know firsthand the power of an open and loving community, where people still wave, still stop to say hello—acknowledging that you exist in the world, that you matter. These are the connections and simple acts of kindness that can and will save lives. I know this to be true, because my community opened its arms and helped save mine.

—BRAD PEACOCK

POET BIOGRAPHIES

JENNIFER L. ABOD, PhD, is an award-winning lesbian feminist documentary filmmaker, former radio broadcaster, talk-show host, and assistant professor of communications and women's studies. When her wife was diagnosed with Alzheimer's, she turned to poetry. She has been published by *ONE ART*, *Artemis Journal*, *Persimmon Tree*, *Metro Weekly*, Silver Birch Press, *Sinister Wisdom*, *Wild Crone Wisdom*, *Fruitslice*, *Discretionary Love*, and *Spillway*. Dr. Abod was the singer in the New Haven Women's Liberation Rock Band from 1970 to 1976. She currently sings jazz in Long Beach, California. Find out more about her work at jenniferabod.com.

KELLI RUSSELL AGODON is a bi/queer poet and editor whose newest book, *Dialogues with Rising Tides* (Copper Canyon Press), was named a finalist in the Washington State Book Awards. She is the cofounder of Two Sylvias Press, where she works as an editor and book cover designer. She recently published *Demystifying the Manuscript: Essays and Interviews on Creating a Book of Poems*, which she coedited with Susan Rich. Kelli lives in a sleepy seaside town in Washington State, where she is an avid paddleboarder and hiker. She teaches at Pacific Lutheran University's low-residency MFA program, the Rainier Writing Workshop. She also cohosts the poetry series Poems You Need with Melissa Studdard. Learn more at agodon.com and twosylviaspress.com.

JAROD K. ANDERSON is the author of three best-selling collections of nature poetry, *Field Guide to the Haunted Forest*, *Love Notes from the Hollow Tree*, and *Leaf Litter*. His memoir, *Something in the Woods*

Loves You (Timber Press/Hachette, 2024), explores his lifelong struggle with depression through a lens of love and gratitude for the natural world. Jarod created and voices *The CryptoNaturalist* podcast, a scripted show about real adoration for fictional wildlife. He lives in Ohio between a park and a cemetery.

BECK ANSON (they/them) blends their queer, trans, and disabled identities into their poetry, published in outlets like *Rattle, RHINO,* and the 2023 *Beyond Queer Words* anthology. Their poem "I Admit Myself to the Psych Ward in a Pandemic" was a finalist for the 2020 Rattle Poetry Prize. They are also the author of the chapbook *Blossom Boy* (Thirty West Publishing House), winner of the seventh annual Wavelengths Chapbook Contest. They reside in western Massachusetts.

CRISTIN O'KEEFE APTOWICZ (she/her) was founding president of Philadelphia's first LGBTQIA+ high school organization: Central High School's Straight and Gay Alliance (SAGA). Straight herself but not wanting fellow club members to be outed, she established the rule that if anyone asked about sexual orientation during their club's monthly bake sales, the standard reply would be, "I'm not allowed to say, but I hear the cookies are bi." Her eighth poetry collection, *Against Vanishing,* is forthcoming in 2026. Find out more at aptowicz.com.

M. J. ARCANGELINI, born in Pennsylvania in 1952, has lived in Northern California since 1979. He has published extensively in magazines and anthologies. Over the years he has done an array of things to keep a roof over his head, some embarrassing or illegal and none of them truly lucrative. He is currently trying, unsuccessfully, to retire. He has six published collections, the most recent of which is *Pawning My Sins* (Luchador Press).

CAMERON AWKWARD-RICH is the author of two collections of poetry: *Sympathetic Little Monster* (Ricochet Editions) and *Dispatch* (Persea Books). Also a scholar of trans theory and expressive culture in the US, Cameron earned his PhD from Stanford University's Program in Modern Thought and Literature. His book *The Terrible We: Thinking with Trans Maladjustment* was published by Duke University Press. Presently, he is an associate professor in the Women, Gender, Sexuality Studies program at the University of Massachusetts Amherst.

HOLLIN BAHN (she/her) is a lesbian, poet, artist, and art therapist who believes in kindness as a warrior practice and in artmaking as alchemy for healing trauma. Hollin has lived for many years in the wild adventure of a disabling chronic illness. Though her soul is canoeing on a mountain lake, she currently lives in the New Mexico desert with her beloved wife and two cats. Read more about her work at hollinbahn.com.

T-M BAIRD'S work has appeared in the *Awake in the World* anthology and *Deep Wild Journal*, among other publications. They write primarily on environmental ethics and mystical poetics. T-M taught toddlers, sold books, and ran a small post office before returning to their native Northeast to focus on growing vegetables with their sweetheart and mixed-breed dog.

ALEGRIA BARCLAY (she/her) is a multiracial queer woman, mother, poet, and educator whose 20-year career is founded upon a commitment to social justice and an abiding belief that creativity, compassion, and communication combined can bring about social change. Having grown up and taught overseas, Alegria is a firm believer in both our shared humanity and our richly complex diversity and believes in inspiring others to exercise their radical imagination to build the Beloved Community.

ELLEN BASS'S most recent collection, *Indigo*, was published by Copper Canyon Press. Her other poetry books include *Like a Beggar*, *The Human Line*, and *Mules of Love*. Her poems appear frequently in the *New Yorker*, the *American Poetry Review*, and many other journals. Among her awards are fellowships from the Guggenheim Foundation, the National Endowment for the Arts, and the California Arts Council, as well as a Lambda Literary Award and three Pushcart Prizes. She teaches in the MFA writing program at Pacific University.

EBEN E. B. BEIN (they/he) is a biology teacher turned climate justice educator at the nonprofit Our Climate. They were a 2022 Fellow for the Writing By Writers workshop and winner of the 2022 Writers Rising Up "Winter Variations" poetry contest. His first chapbook, *Character Flaws,* is out with fauxmoir lit, and he's published with the likes of *Nimrod*, *New Ohio Review*, and *Crab Creek Review*. They are currently completing their first full collection about parent-child estrangement, healing, and love, and they can be found online at ebenbein.com or @ebenbein. He lives on Pawtucket land (Cambridge, Massachusetts) with some houseplants that are not dead because his husband remembers to water them.

KIMBERLY BLAESER (she/her), past Wisconsin Poet Laureate, is the founding director of Indigenous Nations Poets and author of six poetry collections including *Ancient Light, Copper Yearning*, and *Résister en dansant/Ikwe-niimi: Dancing Resistance*. An enrolled member of White Earth Nation, Blaeser is an Anishinaabe activist and environmentalist. An MFA faculty member at the Institute of American Indian Arts and professor emerita at UW–Milwaukee, her accolades include a lifetime achievement award from Native Writers' Circle of the Americas.

RICHARD BLANCO is the fifth presidential inaugural poet in US history—at the time, the youngest person and the first Latino, immigrant, and gay person to serve in this role. Born in Madrid to Cuban exile parents and raised in Miami, Blanco writes poetry characterized by the negotiation of cultural identity and place. He is the author of the poetry collections *Looking for the Gulf Motel*, *Directions to the Beach of the Dead*, and *City of a Hundred Fires*; the poetry chapbooks *Matters of the Sea*, *One Today*, and *Boston Strong*; a children's book of his inaugural poem "One Today," illustrated by Dav Pilkey; and *Boundaries*, a collaboration with photographer Jacob Hessler. His book of poems *How to Love a Country* (Beacon Press) interrogates the American narrative, past and present, and celebrates the still unkept promise of its ideals. He has also authored *Homeland of My Body: New & Selected Poems* and the memoirs *The Prince of Los Cocuyos: A Miami Childhood* and *For All of Us, One Today: An Inaugural Poet's Journey*. He lives with his partner in Bethel, Maine.

SALLY BLIUMIS-DUNN is an associate editor-at-large and features writer for *Plume* and teaches the personal essay at the 92nd Street Y in NYC. Her poems have appeared in *32 Poems*, *New Ohio Review*, *On the Seawall*, the *Paris Review*, *Plume*, *Poetry London*, *Prairie Schooner*, the *New York Times*, *PBS News Hour*, *upstreet*, the *Writer's Almanac*, and the Academy of American Poets' Poem-a-Day. In 2002, she was a finalist for the Nimrod/Hardman Pablo Neruda Prize. Her third full-length collection, *Echolocation*, was published by Plume Editions/Madhat Press and was a finalist for the Eric Hoffer Award as well as the Julie Suk Award.

MICHAEL BLUMENTHAL, formerly director of creative writing at Harvard and professor of law at the West Virginia University College of Law, has taught at universities throughout the world. In addition to 10 books of poetry, most recently *Correcting World: Poems Selected & New, 1980–2024*, he has published a novel, a memoir, short stories, essays, and translations. He spends his time between Washington, DC, and the small Hungarian village of Hegymagas near Lake Balaton.

KENYA BÖES (she/her) is a queer aspiring poet living in central Arkansas with her girlfriend and her tortoiseshell cat, Little Bit. She currently works as an outreach librarian and is pursuing a degree in strategic communications, hoping to continue nonprofit work in the areas of social and environmental justice. When not writing, she enjoys volunteering with the local Pride Alliance to host LGBTQIA+ community events, taking spontaneous road trips, and reading cozy high fantasy.

JESS BOUCHARD (she/her) is a tea-partying, poetry-writing, quirky English teacher turned principal living in southern Vermont with her spouse and their children. When she's not running a school, she leads Queer Connect, an LGBTQIA+ organization empowering youth to live their best and truest lives. She's grateful for this life and journey!

LISA BREGER was the director of the Undergraduate Writing Program at Pine Manor College for many years. Currently, she leads workshops in poetry as a spiritual practice. In 2020, she received the Thomas Merton Award for Poetry of the Sacred, and she was a runner-up for the Ruth Stone Poetry Prize in 2015. She lives by Lake Cochituate with her wife, Anne Parker, and their beloved English setter, Macy Mae.

ANDRÉS LARIOS BROWN (they/elle) is a queer and nonbinary mezcla bella (beautiful mix) of Guatemalan and Western European ancestry. They are a licensed marriage and family therapist, adjunct instructor, and healer. They have devoted their life and career to better understanding healing, hope, and resilience for marginalized people. They focus on queer identity development and healing acute, systemic, and intergenerational trauma for QTBIPOC communities. They live in Utah with their poet husband and in community with beautiful family and friends.

PHILLIP WATTS BROWN (he/him) is the author of *Boy with Flowers in His Mouth* (Gold Line Press). He received an MFA in poetry from Oregon State University, and his poems have appeared in several journals including *Ninth Letter*, *The Common*, *Nimrod*, *Ruminate*, and *Spillway*. He also serves as a poetry editor for the journal *Halfway Down the Stairs*. He and his husband, Andrés, live in Ogden, Utah. Find more of his poetry at phillipwattsbrown.com.

STEPHANIE BURT (she/her) is a poet, literary critic, and professor with nine published books, including two critical books on poetry and three poetry collections. Her essay collection *Close Calls with Nonsense* (Graywolf Press) was a finalist for the National Book Critics Circle Award. Her most recent poetry collection is *We Are Mermaids* (Graywolf Press). Currently, she is a professor of English at Harvard University.

GABRIELLE CALVOCORESSI is the author of the poetry collections *Rocket Fantastic*; *Apocalyptic Swing*, which was a finalist for the 2009 Los Angeles Times Book Prize; and *The Last Time I Saw Amelia Earhart* (all from Persea Books). They are the recipient of numerous awards and fellowships, including a Stegner Fellowship and Jones

Lectureship from Stanford University. Calvocoressi teaches at the University of North Carolina at Chapel Hill and lives in Carrboro, North Carolina.

KAYLEB RAE CANDRILLI (they/them) is a 2019 Whiting Award winner in poetry and the author of *Water I Won't Touch* (Copper Canyon Press), *All the Gay Saints* (Saturnalia), and *What Runs Over* (YesYes Books). Candrilli was a 2017 finalist for the Lambda Literary Award in transgender poetry and a 2017 finalist for the American Book Fest's Best Book Award in LGBTQ Non-fiction. They live in Philadelphia with their partner.

CHRISTEN CAREAGA, a native of Oregon's Willamette Valley, is a longtime educator who loves seeing children, teens, and adults fall in love with writing for the first time. She likes to spend her days drinking copious cups of tea, planning the next travel adventure, and philosophizing till the wee hours with her husband.

GRANT CHEMIDLIN (he/him) is the author of *What We Lost in the Swamp* (Central Avenue Poetry), a finalist for the Lambda Literary Award for gay poetry. Recent poems can be found in *Palette Poetry*, *Quarterly West*, *Tupelo Quarterly*, and *Atlanta Review*, among others. You can learn more about him and his work at grantchemidlin.com.

KAI COGGIN (she/her) is the inaugural poet laureate of the City of Hot Springs, Arkansas, and author of five collections, most recently *Mother of Other Kingdoms* (Harbor Editions). She is a certified master naturalist, a K–12 teaching artist, and host of the longest running consecutive weekly open mic series in the country, Wednesday Night Poetry. She lives with her wife in a peaceful valley, where they tend to wild things and each other.

ELISABETH CRAGO holds an MFA from Carlow University; a BA in English from the University of Michigan; and an MS in nursing from Lehman College, CUNY. A retired nursing administrator, she settled in Pittsburgh, Pennsylvania, in 2014 after living for 12 years in New Zealand. Find her work in *Voices from the Attic*, *Eye to the Telescope*, *Shot Glass Journal*, *Dreamers Creative Writing*, *ONE ART*, and *Dionne's Story*.

JAMES CREWS is the author of numerous prize-winning collections of poetry and the editor of three best-selling poetry anthologies, now appearing as a set titled *A Boxful of Poetry*. He also runs an online writing community called The Monthly Pause (themonthlypause.com) and offers a free weekly newsletter on Substack called *Poetry Is Life*. For more information and news on future projects, visit jamescrews.net.

BARBARA CROOKER is the author of 10 books of poetry, including *Some Glad Morning* (Pitt Poetry Series), longlisted for the Julie Suk Award from Jacar Press; *The Book of Kells*, which won the Best Book of 2019 award from Poetry by the Sea; and *Slow Wreckage* (Grayson Books). She is also a Grammy finalist for spoken word and has received awards such as the Yeats Poetry Prize and the Thomas Merton Prize in Poetry of the Sacred.

JULIE CUMMINGS (she/her) resides in Colorado with her wife, Carla Jordan. She currently serves as the president of Columbine Poets, Inc., and has previously held the position of president of the National Federation of State Poetry Societies. Julie regularly conducts poetry writing workshops and hosts a monthly poetry open mic. Her book of poetry, *Ride of My Life*, is available at juliecummingspoetry.com.

ANNA LUCIA DELOIA (she/her) is a bisexual Italian-American writer, researcher, and educator based in Massachusetts. Her poems have been published in *Rattle*, *Midway Journal*, and the *Paterson Literary*

Review. She is most inspired by working with kids and families, which she does as cocreator of the social justice education initiative Imagining More Just Futures. Read more about her at annaluciakirby.com.

MARGARET DeRITTER is the author of the poetry collection *Singing Back to the Sirens* (Unsolicited Press), which was described by poet Diane Seuss as a collection of "achingly beautiful and gutsy poems" that "represent an autobiography of love." DeRitter also won the 2018 Celery City Chapbook Contest for *Fly Me to Heaven by Way of New Jersey*. She lives in Kalamazoo, Michigan, and serves as copy editor and poetry editor of *Encore* magazine.

ALEX DIMITROV is the author of four books of poetry including *Ecstasy* (Knopf), *Love and Other Poems*, *Together and by Ourselves*, *Begging for It*, and the chapbook *American Boys*. He is Writer in Residence at New York University's Creative Writing Program, and his poems have been published in the *New Yorker*, the *New York Times*, the *Paris Review*, and *Poetry*.

MARK DOTY is the author of nine books of poetry, including *Deep Lane*; *Fire to Fire: New and Selected Poems*, which won the 2008 National Book Award; and *My Alexandria*, winner of the Los Angeles Times Book Prize, the National Book Critics Circle Award, and the T.S. Eliot Prize in the UK. He is also the author of four memoirs: the *New York Times*–bestselling *What Is the Grass*, *Dog Years*, *Firebird*, and *Heaven's Coast*.

RITA DOVE published her first book of poems, *The Yellow House on the Corner*, in 1980. She has followed this work with several other collections, including *Museum*, *Thomas and Beulah*, *Grace Notes*, *Selected Poems*, *Mother Love*, *On the Bus with Rosa Parks*, and *American Smooth*. In 1993, Dove became Poet Laureate of the United States, the first Black poet to receive this honor.

VISVESHWAR ELANGO (he/him) is a polymath with a diverse academic background in engineering, law, and psychology. Beyond his professional endeavors of software engineering and psychotherapy, Visveshwar finds solace and passion in singing, writing, skincare, and maintaining his fitness. In 2023 he debuted his poetry collection, *Boy from the Poems*, resonating with the profound nuances of love and longing from a deeply personal perspective, which adds a unique voice to the rich landscape of love poetry.

JOSHUA JENNIFER ESPINOZA is a trans woman poet. Her work has been featured in *Poetry Magazine*, *The Paris Review*, *The American Poetry Review*, *The Rumpus*, *Poem-a-Day* on poets.org, and elsewhere. She is the author of *I'm Alive / It Hurts / I Love It* (Big Lucks, 2019) and *There Should Be Flowers* (The Accomplices, 2016). She holds an MFA in poetry from UC Riverside and is currently a professor of creative writing. Jennifer lives in California with her wife, poet/essayist Eileen Elizabeth, and their cat and dog.

LAURA FOLEY is a bi/queer poet and author of 10 poetry collections, most recently *Sledding the Valley of the Shadow* (Fernwood Press). She has won a Narrative Prize, the Common Good Books Poetry Prize, the Bisexual Book Award, *Atlanta Review*'s Grand Prize, and others. She and her wife, Clara Giménez, live on the steep banks of the Connecticut River in New Hampshire with their two romping canines.

RUDY FRANCISCO is one of the most recognizable names in spoken word poetry. He was born, raised, and still resides in San Diego, California. As an artist, Rudy Francisco is an amalgamation of social critique, introspection, honesty, and humor. He uses personal narratives to discuss the politics of race, class, gender, and religion while simultaneously pinpointing and reinforcing the interconnected nature of human existence. He is the author of *I'll Fly Away* (Button Poetry).

JENNY GEORGE is the author of *After Image* and *The Dream of Reason* (both from Copper Canyon Press). She works in social justice philanthropy and lives in Santa Fe, New Mexico.

ANDREA GIBSON (they/them/theirs) is a queer author of five collections of poetry, including *Lord of the Butterflies* (Button Poetry), which sold over 20,000 copies worldwide. Winner of the Independent Publishers Book Award in 2019, Andrea is also a three-time Goodreads Choice Awards finalist and was named poet laureate of Colorado in 2024. In 2017, Penguin Books published *Take Me with You*, an illustrated collection of Gibson's most beloved quotes, and in 2019, Chronicle Books published their first nonfiction endeavor, *How Poetry Can Change Your Heart*. Gibson's most recent book is *You Better Be Lightning*.

NIKITA GILL is a British-Indian poet, playwright, writer, and illustrator based in the south of England. Gill's work was first published when she was 12 years old, and she has since published eight volumes of poetry, including *Your Soul Is a River*; *Wild Embers: Poems of Rebellion, Fire, and Beauty*; *Fierce Fairytales: Poems & Stories to Stir Your Soul*; *Great Goddesses: Life Lessons from Myths and Monsters*; *Your Heart Is the Sea*; *The Girl and the Goddess*; *Where Hope Comes From: Poems of Resilience, Healing, and Light*; and *These Are the Words: Fearless Verse to Find Your Voice*.

ANNETTE LANGLOIS GRUNSETH received a Pushcart Prize nomination for her book *Becoming Trans-Parent: One Family's Journey of Gender Transition* and a Gold Medal Award from the Military Writers Society of America for her book *Combat and Campus: Writing Through War*. Her poems have been published by *Amethyst Review*, The Poetry Box, *Poetry of Presence II*, Silver Birch Press, and other places. She also received the Hal Gruetzmacher Poetry Prize in Wisconsin. Learn more at annette -grunseth.com.

JOY HARJO served as the 23rd United States Poet Laureate, the first Native American to hold the position and the only US Poet Laureate to be awarded a third term. Born in Tulsa, Oklahoma, Harjo is an internationally renowned performer and writer of the Muscogee (Creek) Nation. She is the author of nine books of poetry, several plays and children's books, and two memoirs.

CAROLINE HARKINS (she/her) is a queer poet living and writing in the Pacific Northwestern US. She wrote "Golden Hour" for her writing partner the summer they fell in love.

RAGE HEZEKIAH is a Cave Canem, Ragdale, and MacDowell fellow who earned her MFA from Emerson College. Her recent collection, *Yearn*, was a Diode Editions book contest winner and a finalist for the Audre Lorde Award for Lesbian Poetry, the Lambda Literary Award, and the Vermont Book Award. You can find more of her work at ragehezekiah.com.

DONNA HILBERT'S books include *Threnody* and *Enormous Blue Umbrella*, both from Moon Tide Press. Her work has appeared in *Cultural Daily*, *Gyroscope Review*, *Rattle*, *Sheila-Na-Gig*, *ONE ART*, Vox Populi, and anthologies including *The Poetry of Presence*, *The Path to Kindness*, *The Wonder of Small Things*, and *I Thought I Heard a Cardinal Sing*.

AE HINES is the author of two collections, *Adam in the Garden* (Charlotte Lit Press) and *Any Dumb Animal* (Main Street Rag). His poems have appeared in the *Southern Review*, *Rattle*, *The Sun*, *Prairie Schooner*, *New Letters*, *Alaska Quarterly Review*, and many other journals. He received his MFA from Pacific University and teaches poetry for Charlotte Center for Literary Arts. He resides with his husband in Charlotte, North Carolina, and Medellín, Colombia. Read more about him at aehines.net.

LINDA HOGAN is a Chickasaw poet, novelist, essayist, playwright, teacher, and activist who has spent most of her life in Oklahoma and Colorado. Her fiction has garnered many honors, including a Pulitzer Prize nomination, and her poetry collections have received the American Book Award, the Colorado Book Award, and a National Book Critics Circle Award nomination. Her latest book is *A History of Kindness* (Torrey House Press).

JACOB HOROWITZ (he/they) is a playwright and poet based out of Richmond, Virginia. His plays have been performed around the world, but this is his first poem to be published. Jacob likes to write about identity, especially as a transmasculine person, and is thrilled to have their words shared in this collection!

OMOTARA JAMES is the author of the poetry collection *Song of My Softening* (Alice James Books), recommended by NPR, *USA Today*, *Cosmopolitan*, Shondaland, *BOMB* magazine, the *Lambda Literary Review*, *Lavender Magazine*, Book Riot, and *Ms.* magazine. Her chapbook, *Daughter Tongue*, was selected by African Poetry Book Fund (Akashic Books) for the New-Generation African Poets Box Set. Born in Britain, she is the daughter of Nigerian and Trinidadian immigrants. She has lived in England and Scotland and was raised primarily in America.

KYLA JAMIESON (she/her) is a bisexual disabled poet and the author of the collection *Body Count* (Nightwood Editions). Kyla lives and relies on the traditional unceded territories of the Squamish, Musqueam, and Tsleil-Waututh Nations (Vancouver, Canada), where she dreams of systemic change, care-full futures, and disabled joy. Find her online or on a rock next to a river.

ANNE KINSEY (they/them) writes from rural North Carolina, where they live, love, and garden with their queer and interracial family. Anne is a nonprofit founder who is passionate about increasing access to affirming trauma recovery services for the LGBTQIA+ community, as well as for families impacted by human trafficking. Anne is a fat, queer, disabled trauma survivor and avid lover of the outdoors who can be found writing at @anne.kinsey.writes on Instagram or at annekinsey.com.

ANYA KIRSHBAUM (she/her) is a bi/queer poet and somatic therapist living in Seattle, Washington, with her partner and family. Her work has appeared in the *Comstock Review*, *Cirque*, *Mom Egg Review*, *Crannóg*, and *Solstice*, among others. She was a finalist for the New Millennium Writing Awards and was the recipient of the 2023 Banyan Poetry Prize.

ALIX KLINGENBERG is a poet, earth-centered spiritual director, theologian, and visual artist. She is queer and polyamorous and lives in Boston with her family, two black cats, and a ridiculous dog named Cricket.

JOY LADIN (she/her) has published 10 books of poetry, including National Jewish Book Award winner *The Book of Anna* and Lambda Literary Award finalists *Transmigration* and *Impersonation*, as well as a memoir of gender transition and a book of trans theology. Recent works include *Family* and *Once Out of Nature: Selected Essays on the Transformation of Gender*, both from Persea Books. Her writing is available at joyladin.wordpress.com.

JOAN LARKIN is the author of six books of poems, most recently *Old Stranger* (Alice James Books, 2024). Her work in other genres includes *The AIDS Passion; Glad Day: Daily Meditations for Gay, Lesbian, Bisexual, and Transgender People*; and *Sor Juana's Love Poems*, which she translated with Jaime Manrique. Larkin helped found Out & Out Books as part of the feminist literary explosion of the 1970s; coedited the groundbreaking poetry anthologies *Amazon Poetry, Lesbian Poetry*, and *Gay and Lesbian Poetry in Our Time*; and edited *A Woman Like That: Lesbian and Bisexual Writers Tell Their Coming Out Stories*. She currently resides in northern New Jersey.

DORIANNE LAUX'S sixth collection, *Only As the Day is Long: New and Selected Poems*, was a finalist for the 2020 Pulitzer Prize for Poetry, and she is the author most recently of *Life on Earth* (W. W. Norton). *The Book of Men* was awarded the Paterson Prize, and her fourth book of poems, *Facts About the Moon*, won the Oregon Book Award. Laux is the coauthor of the celebrated *The Poet's Companion: A Guide to the Pleasures of Writing Poetry* and author of a new book of prompts, *Finger Exercises for Poets* (W. W. Norton).

LI-YOUNG LEE was born in Djakarta, Indonesia, in 1957 to Chinese political exiles. He is the author of *The Undressing* and *Behind My Eyes* (both from W. W. Norton); *Book of My Nights*, which won the 2002

William Carlos Williams Award; *The City in Which I Love You*, which was the 1990 Lamont Poetry Selection; and *Rose*, which won the Delmore Schwartz Memorial Poetry Award (all from BOA Editions).

PAULA GORDON LEPP (she/her) is a poet from South Charleston, West Virginia, and the proud parent of two daughters—one trans and one gay. Her poetry has appeared in numerous print anthologies and online journals. She is a consultant, educator, and judge for the West Virginia Youth Poet Laureate Program and also curates Garage Door Poetry, a public poetry project in which she displays poems on her own garage door. While not writing poetry, Paula helps operate Bil Lepp Storytelling.

ADA LIMÓN is the author of six poetry collections, including *The Hurting Kind* and *The Carrying*, which won the National Book Critics Circle Award. Her fourth book, *Bright Dead Things,* was named a finalist for the National Book Award, the Kingsley Tufts Poetry Award, and the National Book Critics Circle Award. A recipient of a Guggenheim Fellowship for poetry, she currently serves as US Poet Laureate.

ROB LINNÉ is a professor at Adelphi University, where he directs the Alice Hoffman Young Writers Retreat and serves on the board of the Adelphi Writers and Readers Festival. Recently Rob has published creative nonfiction in *Texas Architect* magazine, *Southern Grit* magazine, and *level:deepsouth*.

TIMOTHY LIU (Liu Ti Mo) was born in 1965 in San Jose, California, to parents from the Chinese mainland. He is the author of *Luminous Debris: New & Selected Legerdemain 1992–2017* (Barrow Street Books); *Kingdom Come: A Fantasia* (Talisman House); *Don't Go Back* to Sleep (Saturnalia); *Polytheogamy* (Saturnalia), and numerous other volumes. He is currently an associate professor at William Paterson University and lives in Manhattan.

AUDRE LORDE (1934–1992) used her writing to shine light on her experience of the world as a Black lesbian woman and later as a mother and person suffering from cancer. A prominent member of the women's and LGBTQ rights movements, her writings called attention to the nature of identity and the ways people from different backgrounds could grow together. She is the author of numerous books, including *Zami: A New Spelling of My Name, The Cancer Journals,* and the prose collection *A Burst of Light.*

KATY LUXEM (she/her) lives in Salt Lake City. She is a graduate of the University of Washington and has a master's degree from the University of Utah. Her work has appeared in *Rattle, McSweeney's, SWWIM Every Day, Rust & Moth, ONE ART, Poetry Online, Appalachian Review,* and others. She is the author of *Until It Is True* (Kelsay Books).

EMILIE LYGREN is a nonbinary poet and outdoor educator whose work emerges from the intersections between scientific observation and poetic wonder. Her first book of poetry, *What We Were Born For,* was selected as a Poetry Foundation Monthly Book Pick in February 2022. Emilie lives in San Rafael, California, where she wonders about oaks and teaches poetry in local classrooms.

JUSTIN MARSH (they/them) is a Vermonter, a proud rural queer, an arts advocate, a state and local political junkie, a published editor, a conservationist, an event organizer, a hobby gardener, a business owner, a public servant, a lover of lists, and one of the state's leading drag performers—Emoji Nightmare. They are happiest when their passions, projects, and identities intersect and blend. They live in Cambridge, Vermont, on the family farm they were raised on, in their late grandparents' home.

CARLING McMANUS lives on a mountainside orchard in West Virginia. Her poems have appeared or are forthcoming in *Frontier Poetry*, *Shenandoah*, *Pleiades*, *Best New Poets*, the *Beloit Poetry Journal,* and other publications. A survivor of conversion therapy, Carling is an outspoken advocate for LGBTQIA+ rights. Read more of her work at carlingmcmanus.com.

TYLER MORTENSEN-HAYES holds an MFA from the University of New Mexico, where he served as poetry editor of *Blue Mesa Review*. His work has appeared in *Frogpond*, *Rattle*, and *Weber—The Contemporary West*. Tyler was longlisted for *Palette Poetry*'s 2023 Rising Poet Prize and is currently at work on his first full-length manuscript. Originally from the Rocky Mountains, he resides in the Pacific Northwest, where he can't stop writing poems about redwoods, crows, and whales.

MARK NEPO is a poet, philosopher, and master teacher who has moved and inspired readers and seekers all over the world through his 26 books, including the number-one *New York Times* bestseller *The Book of Awakening*. Mark is a frequent guest on Oprah Winfrey's *Super Soul Sunday* and his newest book, *You Don't Have to Do It Alone: The Power of Friendship*, celebrates one of the most important aspects of being human: friendship. For information, visit marknepo.com.

ASTRID NEWENHOUSE is a scientist retired from a career in agriculture. She grows oodles of vegetables, fruit, and flowers and enjoys spending time in woods and lakes looking for animals. Astrid embraces queerness, is an activist and a mom, and lives with her husband in Wisconsin.

NAOMI SHIHAB NYE recently served as the Young People's Poet Laureate (Poetry Foundation). Her most recent books are *Everything Comes Next, Collected & New Poems, Cast Away* (poems about trash), *The Tiny Journalist*, and *Voices in the Air: Poems for Listeners*. Her latest book is *Grace Notes: Poems About Families*. She lives in San Antonio, Texas.

JANUARY GILL O'NEIL (she/her) is an associate professor at Salem State University and the author of *Glitter Road, Rewilding, Misery Islands*, and *Underlife*, all published by CavanKerry Press. From 2019 to 2020, she served as the John and Renée Grisham Writer in Residence at the University of Mississippi, Oxford. A Cave Canem fellow, she serves as board chair of AWP and lives in Beverly, Massachusetts.

JASON O'TOOLE (he/him) is poet laureate of North Andover, the cofounder of the Anne Bradstreet Poetry Contest, and the author of two collections and one chapbook of poetry. He is a hospital risk manager north of Boston and treasurer of the Independent Living Resource Center in San Francisco, California.

PÁDRAIG Ó TUAMA is the author of the poetry collections *Kitchen Hymns* (Copper Canyon Press); and *Daily Prayer with the Corrymeela Community, Sorry for Your Troubles*, and *Readings from the Books of Exile*, all published by Canterbury Press in the United Kingdom. He is also the editor of the anthology *Poetry Unbound* (W. W. Norton) and of the memoir *In the Shelter: Finding a Home in the World* (Hodder & Stoughton), a book of spiritual reflection.

BRAD PEACOCK is a veteran, an organic farmer, and a former candidate for the US Senate. He is also an author who has been featured in *Seven Days, VTDigger*, the *Washington Blade*, and the *New York Times*. He lives with his husband on land that he is rehabilitating with native plants and flowers, slowly returning the ecosystem to a paradise for pollinators and all wildlife.

SETH PENNINGTON is a medical social worker and an editor and designer for Sibling Rivalry Press, an independent publishing house based in Little Rock, Arkansas, that he runs with his husband, Bryan Borland. He is the author of *Tertulia*, which was a finalist for the Eric Hoffer Chapbook Award. He is coeditor of *Joy Exhaustible*, editor of *Assaracus* and *Stonewall 50*, and poetry editor of *Equinox*.

CARL PHILLIPS is the author of 16 books of poetry, most recently *Then the War: And Selected Poems 2007–2020* (FSG and Carcanet). His honors include the Pulitzer Prize, the Jackson Poetry Prize, the Aiken Taylor Award in Modern American Poetry, the Kingsley Tufts Poetry Award, a Lambda Literary Award, the PEN/USA Award for Poetry, and fellowships from the Guggenheim Foundation, the Library of Congress, the American Academy of Arts and Letters, and the Academy of American Poets. He teaches at Washington University in St. Louis.

JESSICA E. PIERCE (she/her) is the author of *Consider the Body, Winged* (First Matter Press). Her two expansive children inspire her to embrace herself as a bisexual neurodivergent human committed to educational justice and creative community. You can find her poems in *Bellingham Review*, *Cimarron Review*, *Euphony*, *Painted Bride Quarterly*, and elsewhere. She has been a finalist for CALYX's Poetry Prize, *New Ohio Review*'s NORward Prize, *Nimrod*'s Pablo Neruda Prize for Poetry, and the MVICW poetry contest, for which she received a poet fellowship.

CAROL POTTER'S most recent book of poems, *What Happens Next Is Anyone's Guess,* was awarded the 2021 Pacific Coast Series Award from Beyond Baroque Books. Other books include *Some Slow Bees,* winner of the 2014 Field Poetry Prize from Oberlin College Press; *Otherwise Obedient* (Red Hen Press, 2007), a finalist in the Lambda LGBT awards for 2007; and *Short History of Pets,* which won the 1999 Cleveland State Poetry Center Award and the Balcones Award. She lives in Vermont's Northeast Kingdom.

DAVID B. PRATHER (bisexual—he/him) is the author of three poetry collections: *We Were Birds* (Main Street Rag), *Shouting at an Empty House* (Sheila-Na-Gig Editions), and *Bending Light with Bare Hands* (Fernwood Press). He lives in Parkersburg, West Virginia, and can be found at davidbprather.com.

MINNIE BRUCE PRATT (1946–2023) was an American poet, educator, activist, and essayist. She retired in 2015 from her position as a professor of writing and women's studies at Syracuse University, where she was invited to help develop the university's first LGBT studies program. Her poetry books include *Magnified* (Wesleyan University Press); *The Dirt She Ate: Selected and New Poems* (University of Pittsburgh Press), winner of the Lambda Literary Award for Poetry; and *Crime Against Nature* (Firebrand Books).

ALISON PRINE'S latest collection of poems, *Loss and Its Antonym* (Headmistress Press), won the 2023 Sappho's Prize in Poetry. Her debut poetry collection, *Steel* (Cider Press Review), was named a finalist for the 2017 Vermont Book Award. Her poems have appeared in *Ploughshares*, the *Virginia Quarterly Review*, *Five Points*, *Harvard Review*, *Prairie Schooner*, and other journals. She lives and works in Burlington, Vermont.

PATRICK RAMSAY is a queer, Utah-based poet who was raised along the wetlands of the Great Salt Lake. He studied English and creative writing at Weber State University, where he was editor-in-chief of *Metaphor*. He owns Happy Magpie Book & Quill, an independent, pay-what-you-want bookshop in Ogden, Utah. His poems focus on land, heart, and community in the West. His debut poetry chapbook is *Butterflies Are Rare in Beehives*. Read more at @writepatrick and patrickramsaypoet.com.

ABY RAY is a queer mom, surrogate, advocate, and weirdo who grew up in the San Francisco Bay Area on poetry zines and blackberries right off the bramble. Her poems have been published in *Moist Poetry Journal* and on lampposts around her neighborhood. She feels limerick battles should be used to settle disputes more often.

ADRIENNE RICH (1929–2012) was an American poet, essayist, and activist. Her many collections of poetry include *Diving into the Wreck* and *The Dream of a Common Language*, both from W. W. Norton.

ALEX GRAYSON RIPLEY arrived at an understanding of his transmasculine nonbinary identity in his mid-40s, learning through the example of his two trans kids and the love and support of his wife, Chaya. Alex and Chaya live in picturesque Saint Margaret's Bay, Nova Scotia, with their blended family of assorted pets, plants, and kids.

SHAWN AVENINGO SANDERS'S poems have appeared worldwide in literary journals including *CALYX*, *Eunoia Review*, *Blue Heron Review*, *Tule Review*, *Amsterdam Quarterly*, *About Place Journal,* and *Snapdragon*, to name a few. Author of *What She Was Wearing*, Shawn is cofounder of The Poetry Box and managing editor of the *Poeming Pigeon*. An ally in support of her brilliant gay daughters, she is also mother to an amazing son and grandmother to one darling baby girl.

MOUDI SBEITY (he/they/habibi) is a first-generation graduate student from Lebanon in the Mindfulness Based Transpersonal Counseling Program at Naropa University. Before attending Naropa, Moudi operated a Lebanese restaurant in Utah and was a named plaintiff in the *Kitchen v. Herbert* case that brought marriage equality to the Tenth Circuit states. As a person who stutters, he is passionate about the therapeutic benefits of poetry and writing as practices in self-expression and relational well-being, and they find joy in sharing space with others on the page.

MICHAEL SIMMS (he/him) is a poet, novelist, and LGBTQIA+ ally. His most recent collections of poetry are *Strange Meadowlark* and *Jubal Rising* (Ragged Sky). His most recent speculative novels comprise the Talon Trilogy (Madville). Simms is the founding editor emeritus of Autumn House Press and the founding editor of Vox Populi. In 2011, Simms was awarded a certificate of recognition from the Pennsylvania Legislature for his service to the arts.

DANEZ SMITH (they/them) is the author of three collections including *Homie* and *Don't Call Us Dead*. They have won the Forward Prize for Best Collection, the Minnesota Book Award in Poetry, the Lambda Literary Award for Gay Poetry, and the Kate Tufts Discovery Award, and they have been a finalist for the NAACP Image Award in Poetry, the National Book Critics Circle Award, and the National Book Award. Danez's poetry and prose have been featured in *Vanity Fair*, the *New York Times*, the *New Yorker*, *GQ*, and *Best American Poetry*, and on *The Late Show with Stephen Colbert*. They live in Minneapolis near their people.

NATHAN SPOON is an autistic poet with learning disabilities. He is the author of *The Importance of Being Feeble-Minded* (Nine Mile Books), and his poems and essays have appeared in the Academy of American Poets' Poem-a-Day, the *American Poetry Review*, *Bennington Review*, *Gulf Coast*, *Poetry*, the *Southern Review*, and *swamp pink*, as well as in the anthologies *The American Sonnet: An Anthology of Poems and Essays*, *How to Love the World: Poems of Gratitude and Hope*, *Mid/South Sonnets: A Belle Point Press Anthology*, and *The Wonder of Small Things: Poems of Peace and Renewal*. He is editor of *Queerly*.

BRENNAN STAFFIERI (they/them) is a nonbinary poet born and raised in the Pacific Northwest. They completed their MFA in creative writing with Pacific University. They are a former intern with CALYX Press, where they were in charge of developing queer workshops and pro-gramming for the press. Their work has appeared in *oddball magazine* and on Portland stages. They live in Portland, Oregon, with their wife and partner. They can be found on Instagram @BrennanLikesYou.

MAYA STEIN is the current poet laureate of Belfast, Maine. She has kept a weekly short-form poetry practice, 10-Line Tuesday, since 2005, and facilitates writing workshops in person and online. She lives with her wife and three rescue cats in a house named Toad Hall and is the editorial director of Toad Hall Editions, a small press publishing the work of women and gender-diverse writers and art-ists. Visit mayastein.com for more information.

JACQUELINE SUSKIN (she/they) has composed over 40,000 improvisational poems with her ongoing writing project, Poem Store. Suskin is the author of eight books, including *Help in the Dark Season* and *A Year in Practice*. An ecstatic earth-worshiper, she is married to the planet and to Eric F. Johnson-Acevedo, a human being. Her gen-der is fluid and infinite. She spent years gardening, living, and learning at Fancyland, a rural, queer land project in Northern California.

PAUL TRAN is the author of the debut poetry collection *All the Flowers Kneeling*, published by Penguin. Their work appears in the *New York Times*, the *New Yorker*, *Best American Poetry*, and elsewhere. Winner of the Discovery/*Boston Review* Poetry Prize, as well as fellowships from the Poetry Foundation, Stanford University, and the National Endowment for the Arts, Paul is an assistant professor of English and Asian American studies at the University of Wisconsin–Madison.

ROSEMERRY WAHTOLA TROMMER cohosts *Emerging Form* (a creative process podcast), Secret Agents of Change (a surreptitious kindness cabal), and Soul Writer's Circle. Her daily audio series, the *Poetic Path*, is on the Ritual app for your phone. Her poetry has appeared on *PBS News Hour* and the Carnegie Hall stage. Her poetry collections include *All the Honey* and *The Unfolding*. Her one-word mantra is: adjust. Find more information at wordwoman.com.

LAURA WARD (she/her) is a licensed marriage and family therapist and a fellow in Thanatology. She works in hospice, providing grief counseling and as the manager of psychosocial services. Laura is a voracious reader, dedicated seeker of knowledge, and someone who is deeply committed to her own personal growth. She is endlessly fascinated by humans, nature, and the cosmos, weaving these interests, as well her own personal experiences, into poetry. Laura, her wife, triplet teenagers, corgi, and cat reside in upstate New York.

EMMA WYNN (they/them) is a queer, nonbinary poet and author of *The World Is Our Anchor* (FutureCycle Press). They teach philosophy, LGBTQIA+ US history, and psychology at a boarding high school in Connecticut, where they live with their partner, two children, and dogs. You can read more about her work at emmawynnpoetry.com.

BIANCA AMIRA ZANELLA (she/they) is a queer, award-winning poet on the unceded land of the Abenaki. Her poems have appeared in *Writing by Heart*, the *Artful Mind*, and the *Mountain Troubadour*; she's exhibited at Merwin Gallery and Stone Valley Arts. Zanella serves her community as a poetic medicine healer, multidisciplinary artist, and advocate for survivors of violence. As the Paper Poet, she designs experiences to decrease hardship while increasing heartship.

YVONNE ZIPTER (she/her/hers) is author of the poetry collections *The Wordless Lullaby of Crickets*, *Kissing the Long Face of the Greyhound*, *The Patience of Metal* (Lambda Literary Award finalist), and *Like Some Bookie God*; the Russian historical novel *Infraction*; and the nonfiction books *Diamonds Are a Dyke's Best Friend* and *Ransacking the Closet*. Her individual published poems are sold in two repurposed toy-vending machines in Chicago to help fund a local nonprofit organization.

ACKNOWLEDGMENTS

I would like to thank all of the contributors for making this beautiful book a reality. It is beyond humbling to have a dream and watch it come to life. Thank you to all at Storey Publishing for believing in this project, especially Hannah Fries, who really is a rockstar. None of this would have been possible without the love and support of my family and friends. Thank you Mom, Dad, Diane, Erin, and DJ; may we always have each other's backs. To Becca Knouss, I am in awe of you and your passion. You give me hope to keep reaching. To Christy Nevius and Michael Biddy, for always sharing your home, the countless dinners, saunas, and many epic Scrabble games I will always cherish. To my Clear Brook Farm family throughout 20 years of farming, so many of you have enhanced my life. In memory of Phil Herbert, and to his husband, Bob Fogelgren, my gay "dads" who helped pave the way for all of us in the LGBTQIA+ family by always being their authentic selves. To Beth, for helping me heal and gather the tools I need to walk through life more lightly. To my beloved community of Shaftsbury, Vermont, for opening your arms and truly giving me a place to call home. Lastly, I would like to thank my husband, James Crews, not only for your continuous love, but also for always believing in and encouraging me. I would not be the man I am today without you.

— Brad Peacock

I can't thank the amazing team at Storey Publishing enough for their years of unwavering support for anthologies like these, especially Deborah Balmuth, who has retired, and Margaret Lennon, who recently stepped in as publisher. We are both beyond grateful to the many poets who sent us wonderful poems we simply did not have the room to include, and we thank those contributors who generously offered us their work, often at no charge. I'd like to thank my first poetry teacher and mentor, the late David Clewell, for starting me off on anthologies more than two decades ago, giving me an excuse to get lost in the stacks of the library; and Ted Kooser, who has more recently supported all my efforts. Thanks to the many folks who have already made this book a thing of beauty, especially Lisa Congdon for gorgeous art throughout and a wondrous cover; and Richard Blanco for a pitch-perfect foreword. It was a gift to work with my husband, Brad Peacock, on this book, and it is a gift to have built a life with him. We are living proof for anyone who believes that true love might be impossible for them.

— James Crews

CREDITS

Agodon, Kelli Russell, "The Secret Is That the World Loves You." Printed with permission of the author. The title of this poem comes from a line from the poem "Lottery" by Laura Kasischke.

Anderson, Jarod K., "Woodland You" by Jarod K. Anderson. Originally published in *Field Guide to the Haunted Forest*. Reprinted with permission of the author.

Aptowicz, Cristin O'Keefe, "Isn't Every Love Poem an Unfinished Love Poem?" by Cristin O'Keefe Aptowicz, from *How to Love the Empty Air* (Write Bloody Publishing, 2018). Reprinted with permission of the author.

Awkward-Rich, Cameron, "Cento Between the Ending and the End" from *Dispatch*. Copyright © 2019 by Cameron Awkward-Rich. Used by permission of Persea Books, Inc. (New York), www.perseabooks.com. All rights reserved.

Bass, Ellen, "Sleeping With You" from *Mules of Love*. Copyright © 2002 by Ellen Bass. Reprinted with the permission of The Permissions Company, LLC on behalf of BOA Editions, Ltd., boaeditions.org.

Berry, Wendell, "Our Children, Coming of Age" from *New Collected Poems*. Copyright © 1982 by Wendell Berry. Reprinted with the permission of The Permissions Company, LLC on behalf of Counterpoint Press, counterpointpress .com. "The Peace of Wild Things" from *The Peace of Wild Things* by Wendell Berry, published by Penguin. Copyright © Wendell Berry, 1964, 1968, 1970, 1973, 1977, 1980, 1982, 1994, 1999, 2005, 2016. Reprinted by permission of Penguin Books Limited.

Blanco, Richard, "My Father, My Hands" from *Looking for the Gulf Motel* by Richard Blanco, copyright © 2012 by Richard Blanco. Reprinted by permission of the University of Pittsburgh Press.

Brown, Phillip Watts, "Neighbors" by Phillip Watts Brown, originally published in *Up the Staircase Quarterly* and in *Boy with Flowers in His Mouth* (Gold Line Press, 2025). Reprinted with permission of the author.

Burt, Stephanie, "Prayer for Werewolves" from *We Are Mermaids*. Copyright © 2022 by Stephanie Burt. Used with the permission of The Permissions Company, LLC on behalf of Graywolf Press, www.graywolfpress.org.

Calvocoressi, Gabrielle, "She Ties My Bow Tie" from *Rocket Fantastic*. Copyright © 2018 by Gabrielle Calvocoressi. Used by permission of Persea Books, New York. All rights reserved.

Candrilli, Kayleb Rae, "Summer in Wildwood, NJ" from *Water I Won't Touch*. Copyright © 2021 by Kayleb Rae Candrilli. Reprinted with the permission of

Laux, Dorianne, "Enough Music" from *What We Carry*. Copyright © 1994 by Dorianne Laux. Reprinted with the permission of The Permissions Company, LLC on behalf of BOA Editions Ltd., boaeditions.org.

Lee, Li-Young, "One Heart" from *Book of My Nights*. Copyright © 2001 by Li-Young Lee. Reprinted with the permission of The Permissions Company, LLC on behalf of BOA Editions, Ltd., boaeditions.org.

Limón, Ada, "On a Pink Moon" from *The Carrying*. Copyright © 2018 by Ada Limón. Reprinted with the permission of The Permissions Company, LLC on behalf of Milkweed Editions, milkweed.org and the Licensor through PLSclear.

Liu, Timothy, "On a Hill at Night in a Chair Under Stars" from *Vox Angelica*. Copyright © 1992 by Timothy Liu. Reprinted with the permission of The Permissions Company, LLC on behalf of Alice James Books, alicejamesbooks.org.

Lorde, Audre, "Love Poem" from *The Collected Poems of Audre Lorde* by Audre Lorde, © 1975 by Audre Lorde. Used by permission of W. W. Norton & Company, Inc.

Luxem, Katy, "Worship" by Katy Luxem, from *Until It Is True*, published by Kelsay Books 2023. Reprinted with permission of the author.

Lygren, Emilie, "How I want to be beautiful" by Emilie Lygren, published in *Green Shoe Sanctuary*. "Chrysalis" was commissioned by and appears on the wall of a meditation room at the Ohana Center for Child and Adolescent Behavioral Health.

Nye, Naomi Shihab, "So Much Happiness" from *Words Under the Words: Selected Poems* by Naomi Shihab Nye, copyright © 1994. Courtesy of Far Corner Books.

O'Neil, January Gill, "Be Mine" by January Gill O'Neil, originally published in *Couplet Poetry*. Reprinted by permission of the author.

O'Toole, Jason, "Father's Day" by Jason O'Toole, from *The Strange Misgivings of the Sadly Gifted*, DiWulf Publishing House (forthcoming).

Ó Tuama, Pádraig, "The Facts of Life" from *Sorry For Your Troubles* by Pádraig Ó Tuama is © 2018 by Pádraig Ó Tuama. Published by Canterbury Press. Used with permission of the poet.

Phillips, Carl, "Just the Wind for a Sound, Softly" from *Silverchest* by Carl Phillips. Copyright © 2013 by Carl Phillips. Reprinted by permission of Farrar, Straus and Giroux. All Rights Reserved.

Potter, Carol, "Migration" from *Otherwise Obedient*. Copyright © 2008 by Carol Potter. Reprinted with the permission of The Permissions Company, LLC on behalf of Red Hen Press, redhen.org.

Pratt, Minnie Bruce, "Sweet, Sweat" from *Magnified* © 2021 by Minnie Bruce Pratt. Published by Wesleyan University Press, Middletown, CT. Used with permission.

Prine, Alison, "Coming Out" by Alison Prine, first appeared in *Hunger Mountain*. "Far North" first appeared in *Ploughshares*. Reprinted with permission of author.

Ray, Aby, "Groundwork" by Aby Ray, previously published in *Dipity Literary Magazine* online, March 2024.

Rich, Adrienne, Poem III from "Twenty-One Love Poems," from *The Dream of a Common Language: Poems 1974–1977* by Adrienne Rich. Copyright © 1978 by W. W. Norton & Company, Inc. Used by permission of W. W. Norton & Company, Inc.

Simms, Michael, "Sunstar" by Michael Simms originally published in *Rune*. "Sunstar" and "More" by Michael Simms both appeared in *Jubal Rising* (Ragged Sky, 2024). Reprinted with permission of the author.

Smith, Danez, "king the color of space/tower of molasses & marrow" by Danez Smith published in *[insert] boy*, YesYes Books, 2015. Reproduced with permission of Danez Smith and YesYes Books.

Spoon, Nathan, "Ask Me Later" by Nathan Spoon originally appeared in *Zoeglossia, Poem of the Week* and *The Importance of Being Feeble-Minded* from Nine Mile Books. Reprinted with permission of the author.

Stein, Maya, "what to love when you're running out of things to love" by Maya Stein, originally appeared in her weekly newsletter, Ten-Line Tuesday, July 2023.

Suskin, Jacqueline, "Heart Rock" by Jacqueline Suskin, from *The Edge of the Continent Volume One - The Forest* (Write Bloody Publishing). Reprinted with permission of the author.

Tran, Paul, "Enlightenment" from *All the Flowers Kneeling* by Paul Tran, copyright © 2022 by Paul Tran. Used by permission of Penguin Books, an imprint of Penguin Publishing Group, a division of Penguin Random House LLC and Penguin Books Limited. All rights reserved.

Trommer, Rosemerry Wahtola, "Love," by Rosemerry Wahtola Trommer, from *Hush* (Middle Creek Press, 2020). "Watching My Friend Pretend Her Heart Isn't Breaking," from *All the Honey* (Samara Press, 2023). Reprinted with permission of the author.

Wynn, Emma, "On C Block" by Emma Wynn, originally published in *2020 Anthology of Featured Poets*, Moonstone Press (January 2021) and *The World Is Our Anchor*, FutureCycle Press (2023).

Zipter, Yvonne, "Naiad" by Yvonne Zipter was originally published in *ONE ART: a journal of poetry* (June 2022).

All other poems are printed with permission of the authors.

The mission of Storey Publishing is to serve our customers by publishing practical information that encourages personal independence in harmony with the environment.

EDITED BY Hannah Fries
ART DIRECTION AND BOOK DESIGN BY HK Goldstein
ILLUSTRATIONS BY © Lisa Congdon

TEXT © 2025 by James Crews and Brad Peacock
FOREWORD BY Richard Blanco/© Storey Publishing

Storey books may be purchased in bulk for business, educational, or promotional use. Special editions or book excerpts can also be created to specification. For details, please contact your local bookseller or the Hachette Book Group Special Markets Department at special.markets@hbgusa.com.

STOREY PUBLISHING
210 MASS MoCA Way
North Adams, MA 01247
storey.com

Storey Publishing is an imprint of Workman Publishing, a division of Hachette Book Group, Inc., 1290 Avenue of the Americas, New York, NY 10104. The Storey Publishing name and logo are registered trademarks of Hachette Book Group, Inc.

ISBNs: 978-1-63586-895-1 (paperback with flaps); 978-1-63586-896-8 (ebook)

Printed in the United States by Versa Press (interior) and PC (cover) on paper from responsible sources
10 9 8 7 6 5 4 3 2
VER

Library of Congress Cataloging-in-Publication Data on file